DATE DUE

D1403342

PERSPECTIVES

A Multicultural Portrait of

Immigration

By Petra Press

BENCHMARK BOOKS

MARSHALL CAVENDISH

NEW YORK

Cover: An artist's impression of a scene aboard a ship as it enters the harbor of nineteenth-century New York City with its precious cargo of immigrants. Despite the enslavement of Africans, the subjugation of its Native population, and the hardships and hostility that greeted most people whose cultures, languages, and looks were "different," the United States has long represented a haven from oppressive conditions in other parts of the world. From the early 1800s on, the U.S. population has been fed in large part by several great "waves" of immigrants. Also contributing to the population and character of the United States have been the smaller but significant numbers of immigrants, most of them in the twentieth century, from Asia, Africa, Europe, the Middle East, and the Americas.

Benchmark Books
Marshall Cavendish Corporation
99 White Plains Road
Tarrytown, New York 10591-9001, U.S.A.

© Marshall Cavendish Corporation, 1996

Edited, designed, and produced by Water Buffalo Books, Milwaukee

Picture Credits: © The Bettmann Archive: Cover, 6-7, 8, 10, 11, 12, 13, 14, 18, 27, 32, 35, 37, 41, 42; © Steven Ferry: 66; © Beryl Goldberg: 72; © Hazel Hankin: 16, 23, 44; © Reuters/Bettmann: 52, 55; © Franco Salmoiraghi/Photo Resource Hawaii: 56; Courtesy of Robert Stegelmann: 26; © UPI/Bettmann: 24, 28, 31, 34, 38, 39, 40, 43, 46, 48, 49, 51, 53, 59, 60, 62, 63, 65, 68, 69, 71, 74, 75

Library of Congress Cataloging-in-Publication Data

Press, Petra.
    A multicultural portrait of immigration / by Petra Press.
       p.   cm. -- (Perspectives)
    Includes bibliographical references and index.
    Summary: Presents the history of immigration to the United States from around the world beginning with the Indians.
    ISBN 0-7614-0055-9 (lib. bdg.)
    1. United States--Emigration and immigration--History--Juvenile literature. 2. Immigrants--United States--History--Juvenile literature. [1. Immigrants. 2. United States--Emigration and immigration--History.] I. Title. II. Series: Perspectives (Marshall Cavendish Corporation)
    JV6450.P74   1995
    304.8'0973--dc20
                                      95-16876
                                        CIP
                                        AC

To PS – MS

Printed in Malaysia
Bound in the U.S.A.

CONTENTS

About *Perspectives*

Perspectives is a series of multicultural portraits of events and topics in U.S. history. Each volume examines these events and topics not only from the perspective of the white European-Americans who make up the majority of the U.S. population, but also from that of the nation's many people of color and other ethnic minorities, such as African-Americans, Asian-Americans, Hispanic-Americans, and American Indians. These people, along with women, have been given little attention in traditional accounts of U.S. history. And yet their impact on historical events has been great.

The terms *American Indian, Native American, Hispanic-American, Latino, Anglo-American, Black, African-American,* and *Asian-American,* like *European-American* and *white,* are used by the authors in this series to identify people of various national origins. Labeling people is a serious business, and what we call a group depends on many things. For example, a few decades ago it was considered acceptable to use the words *colored* or *Negro* to label Americans of African origin. Today, these words are outdated and often a sign of ignorance or outright prejudice. Some even consider *Black* less acceptable than *African-American* because it focuses on a person's skin color rather than national origins. And yet *Black* has many practical uses, especially to describe people whose origins are not only African but Caribbean or Latin American as well.

If we must label people, it is better to be as specific as possible. That is a goal of *Perspectives* — to be as precise and fair as possible in the labeling of people by race, ethnicity, national origin, or other factors, such as gender, sexual orientation, or disability. When necessary and possible, Americans of Mexican origin will be called *Mexican-Americans.* Americans of Irish origin will be called *Irish-Americans,* and so on. The same goes for American Indians: When possible, specific Indians are identified by their tribal names, such as *Winnebago* or *Mohawk.* But in a discussion of various Indian groups, tribal origins may not always be entirely clear, and so it may be more practical to use *American Indian,* a term that has widespread use among Indians and non-Indians alike.

Even within a group, individuals may disagree over the labels they prefer for their group: *Black* or *African-American? American Indian* or *Native American? Hispanic* or *Latino? White, Anglo,* or *European-American?* Different situations often call for different labels. The labels used in *Perspectives* represent an attempt to be fair, accurate, and perhaps most importantly, to be mindful of what people choose to call *themselves.*

A Note About *Immigration*

It would be hard to discuss U.S. immigration without writing the entire history of the United States. Many historians believe that the Indians who greeted the first Europeans were themselves descendants of people who tens of thousands of years ago migrated to North America over land now covered by the Bering Strait. That would mean that everyone in the U.S. is either an immigrant or the descendant of one. Other historians argue that the Native presence in North America came about over so many thousands of years that it cannot be called a kind of immigration. In any event, writing about the contributions all of our ancestors have made over the centuries would obviously be a subject much too vast to cover in one book. (The hundreds of Native cultures alone would require an entire encyclopedia.)

This book, therefore, will focus on a narrower definition of U.S. immigrants. We will cover in passing the Native Americans, the early European colonists and explorers, and the Africans, both slave and free, who were here before the Declaration of Independence was signed. The bulk of this book, however, will focus on people who came to the United States once it became a nation.

We will show how not everyone came by choice (African and Chinese slaves, for example) and how even among those who did, most were not always welcomed with open arms. One of the sad ironies of the American experience lies in the fact that members of virtually every immigrant group, once having gotten over the hatred they first faced, have promptly resented and discriminated against the ethnic groups that arrived after they did, often to the point of violence. Yet the diversity so many people still find alarming is exactly what has made this nation as strong and vital as it is today.

While each immigrant group had its own unfamiliar language and traditions, wherever they came from, the one thing most had in common was their dream of a better life for themselves and their children. Of course, the idea of "a better life" often meant different things to different people. To some, it meant getting rich quickly and then returning to their homelands; for others, it meant starting a new life in a country where they at least had a fighting chance to escape the desperate cycle of poverty their own countries had guaranteed them. For many, a better life meant freedom from religious persecution or a refuge from political tyranny. Others came to escape famine, disease, or overpopulation.

The great majority of immigrants were plain people whose contributions, if taken individually, might not seem particularly impressive. Yet together, their hard work and innovation helped develop a new nation's industry, commerce, and agriculture and create a thriving, culturally diverse democracy. As the following chapters will show, contrary to what has often been popular belief, immigrant groups are not infested with criminals; they do not bring diseases; and they do not categorically reject our culture. Nor do they refuse to learn English and assimilate, steal our jobs, or drain our resources. As studies and experience continue to demonstrate, they contribute far more to this country — economically, politically, and culturally — than they could ever cost it.

A sick and weary shipload of Pilgrims lands at the Plymouth Colony in 1620,
grateful that their grueling five-week sea voyage is finally over.

CHAPTER ONE

From Colonies to Nation

Agnes, like all the other young women on deck, hung onto the ship's smooth railing as a drowning man hangs onto a floating log. Built in 1670, this may have been one of His Majesty's newest and finest sailing vessels, but it smelled as old and squalid as Noah's Ark must have smelled after forty days at sea. She vowed that if she survived this trip — and by God she *would* survive — she would never set foot in so much as a rowboat again. Agnes breathed in the cold ocean air as deeply as she could, weak from hunger but (thank God) no longer nauseated. She pulled at the frayed, filthy end of one of her braids and sobbed aloud in despair. What Jamestown man would want her for a wife now, looking and smelling like this? No bath or change of clothes in weeks. A good twenty pounds lighter from seasickness. Skin as pasty as buttermilk from lack of air and decent food. She was only seventeen but was sure she looked forty.

Agnes stared into the rolling waves, trying to prolong her short stay on deck. They had been at sea for twenty-two days, and this was only the fourth time she had been allowed up on deck for a breath of fresh air. She almost wished she had stayed home to hoe potatoes with her younger sisters. She was sick to death of this boat and all the other filthy passengers. She was sick of their constant complaining, sick of the spreading disease and the hunger, and sick of the suffocating stench of urine and vomit.

A cold, salty wind whipped at her long skirts, but Agnes did not mind. Two more girls in her section of the hold had died of fever during the night — Mary, the shy Irish girl with all the freckles, and Lizbeth, the older, stuck-up one who kept boasting about all her boyfriends. The crew just tossed their bodies overboard as if they were nothing more than buckets of slop. Well, what did they expect, making five girls share a single, tiny bunk, then cramming forty bunks (twenty upper and twenty lower) into a candle-lit black hole two floors below deck? How many other cells did this old ship hold? How many more women would die before they reached Jamestown?

Agnes felt a tap on her shoulder. It was time to follow the matron back into the hold.

Colonists, Not Immigrants

Immigrants are people who come into an existing country with the intent to settle there permanently. Colonists, like Agnes, on the other hand, are the original settlers or founders of a colony, usually in a distant territory belonging to the mother country. Colonists remain citizens of (and loyal to) their homeland. Therefore, the people who originally settled in North America in the fifteenth, sixteenth, and seventeenth centuries were for the most part colonists, not immigrants, even though they sailed to the Americas from a number of different European countries.

By the mid-eighteenth century, however, North American colonists began to take on a new national identity. They no longer thought of themselves as British (or Dutch, German, Scotch-Irish, or French) but as a group of people who brought together elements from all their various ethnic groups to form a new, very different, and distinctly "American" culture. The European colonists still had their differences, but they were willing to unite together, and by the 1770s they joined forces to fight for their independence. They created a new nation they hoped would be based on the principles of freedom and equality

Baltimore leaders conduct a town planning meeting with their surveyor in 1730. Until early towns enacted sewage, sanitation, and fire laws, urban garbage disposal systems consisted of hogs that roamed the streets eating garbage, and wooden houses and shops were usually built so close together that they practically invited the many fires that often destroyed half the town or more.

for everyone. (Their definition of "everyone," however, did not include such unwilling members of colonial society as African slaves, American Indians, and white indentured servants.)

Even though these ideals have not always been realized, this new nation became the logical haven for refugees from all over the world, people hoping to escape poverty, political upheaval, famine, natural disasters, and religious persecution. To understand the country's tremendous ethnic diversity and the reason so many thousands of immigrants have chosen the United States for their new homeland, it is important to know something about the country's original colonial founders and the reasons they chose to settle in the Americas.

Spanish and Portuguese Conquerors: Taking the Lead

The Spanish and Portuguese were so far ahead in the colonization race that between the two of them, they had carved out the most desirable parts of the Western Hemisphere for themselves — long before England, Holland, and France got more than a toehold. The Spanish empire stretched from the West Indies, across the Caribbean Sea through Mexico, and down to the very tip of South America. The Portuguese (who also had colonies in Africa and the East Indies) claimed the rich, expansive territory of Brazil.

The first colonists from Spain and Portugal were mostly men, either conquering *conquistadors* or Catholic missionaries. The conquistadors seized gold and silver from the Incas and Aztecs and shipped home tons of West Indian sugar. By 1574 (thirty-three years before the first British settlers even started colonizing), there were already about two hundred Spanish cities and towns in North and South America, with over 160,000 Spanish inhabitants (mostly men). By that time, the Spanish had also enslaved over 5 million Indians. And they did all this (they claimed) in the name of Jesus and their Catholic faith.

The greatest impact Spanish colonists had on future U.S. territory was along the southwestern frontier, but by 1610, only a few hundred Spaniards (most of them missionaries) had actually moved into New Mexico. They did not consider the area to be rich enough in either natural resources or Indian civilizations to be worth exploiting. By 1770, the Spanish were pushing out of Mexico toward California, where Jesuits like Junípero Serra set up missions to convert (and exploit) California Indians, but very few other Spanish colonists settled in the area. Spain also maintained military outposts in Florida for a time.

English Settlers Form Colonizing Companies

When the king of England finally authorized North American colonization in the mid-1600s, England was not yet unified enough to have either the money to sponsor new settlements or the military force (like Spain's conquistadors) to "conquer" its new territories. Nor did England have leagues of Catholic missionaries to send. With the recent Protestant upheaval, Catholicism had been

Picturesque Spanish names

The influence of Spanish explorers is most apparent in the Southwest, where cities, towns, mountain ranges, rivers, lakes, and hundreds of other places have Spanish names. There are over four hundred cities and towns in California alone with Spanish-origin names. While its origin is Spanish, Los Angeles is not the original name of that California town. It was shortened from *El Pueblo de Nuestra Señora la Reina de Los Angeles de la Porciuncula*, "The Town of Our Lady, Queen of the Angels of the Porciuncula." California itself is named for an imaginary island in Spanish folklore, meaning "an earthly paradise."

Although many of its members were devout Puritans, the Jamestown colony was established by the Virginia Company in 1607 strictly for commercial reasons. Hundreds of colonists (mostly single young men) died in the first few years from disease and starvation. It was only when they learned to plant tobacco that the colony began to make a profit.

reduced to a minority force in England, which left few Catholic missionaries willing and available to colonize other countries. Instead, England's first colonists were members of chartered companies authorized by the king to establish settlements along North America's Atlantic coast.

People formed and joined British colonizing companies for two main reasons: to get rich and to escape religious persecution. While the commercial companies recruited mostly young males to work in the colonies for a few years and then return to England, religious companies recruited whole families with members of all ages — and recruited them to settle in the colonies permanently.

Jamestown, established by the Virginia Company in 1607, is an example of a strictly commercial colony, while the Plymouth colony, established in Massachusetts in 1620, is an example of a religious colony. (Plymouth was settled by Pilgrims, a group of extremely conservative Puritans who had been so upset at the slow progress of the Protestant Reformation in England that they left the country.) Many colonies, like the Catholic settlement established by Lord Baltimore in Maryland in 1620, were set up as both commercial and religious settlements.

Whatever their reasons for coming, everyone involved in setting up a new British colony had to do his or her share of the backbreaking work. This did not make them equals, however. The elite settlers were the wealthy merchants, planters, and professional men. The huge middle class — the backbone of the colonies — was made up of *yeomen*, farmers who owned small and medium-sized farms, artisans, and smaller tradespeople. Then came white indentured servants and finally, on the bottom of the social ladder, African slaves.

Although almost everyone worked hard to build a new settlement, there was always far more work than people available to do it. One solution was to import white indentured servants from England: debtors, convicts, and other desperate people willing to sell themselves into four to seven years of servitude for a chance to start a new life in the Americas. By 1775, there were over 250,000 of them in the colonies. But once they became free men, many indentured servants learned trades, acquired land, or became successful merchants themselves.

The other solution was to kidnap and import *unwilling* colonists to do the work: African slaves. Although most Africans (and generations of their descendants) were not released from their servitude after a certain number of years and instead remained slaves, some were taught trades like bricklaying, tanning, and carpentry, which gave them just slightly more social status than the Black slaves who were relegated to field labor.

By the early 1700s, the British had established colonies from fishing villages in Nova Scotia to cotton and tobacco plantations in Georgia, North and South Carolina, and Virginia. But the British were not the only early colonists in North America.

Dutch and Swedish Colonists

New Netherlands and New Sweden were founded as coastal trading posts between Britain's Chesapeake Bay (present-day Maryland) and Massachusetts Bay colonies. Dutch and Swedish colonists were mostly merchants and fur traders who wanted to get rich and then return to Europe. Neither Holland

The vast territory stretching from the Appalachians west to the Pacific was a rich source for the fox, beaver, and other furs that brought high prices on the European market. In the 1700s, English and French traders competed to exploit the continent's interior while the Russians scrambled to control the fur trade along the Pacific Northwest Coast.

nor Sweden could get many of their countrymen to settle in North America permanently, however, so both recruited foreigners as colonists. The mix of Dutch, Swedes, Finns, Sephardic Jews, Africans (both free and slave), and even French Huguenots (among others) gave these colonies the diverse ethnic flavor they still have today. The Dutch absorbed the struggling Swedish settlement (now part of Delaware) in about 1660. Dutch colonial lands, in turn, were absorbed by the British in 1664, mainly because of the ongoing difficulties of obtaining enough colonists to do the work. The English changed the name of Holland's best-remembered colony from New Netherlands to New York (now New York state).

The French

After explorer Jacques Cartier staked out areas that included what are now the Canadian cities of Quebec and Montreal for France (in 1535), France's King Louis XIV provided the military and financial support to help expand this territory they named New France. The French also sailed into the Gulf of Mexico and staked their claim to the area around New Orleans. In 1679, an explorer named Robert Cavelier de La Salle proved that the two French territories (Canada in the north and New Orleans in the south) could be united by way of a water route formed by the Great Lakes and Mississippi River. In the next half-century, the French built a line of fortified outposts along that waterway to maintain control of the lands around it they now called the Louisiana Territory and to exploit the fur trade within that territory. They also sent explorers and Jesuit Catholic missionaries by river to penetrate deep into the western regions of the North American continent.

Mountain men in the late 1700s and early 1800s survived hardship to find the richest areas for trapping furs. In the process, their explorations opened up vast areas of territory for new immigrant settlers.

The French failed to maintain their colonial hold in North America because they never made the effort to populate their settlements the way the English did. For the most part, the Frenchmen who sailed to the Americas were more interested in furs than colonization, and by 1754 there were only about fifty-five thousand Frenchmen in North America, most of them fur traders, compared to over one million British colonists.

In 1803, several years after the formation of the United States, the new U.S. government purchased the entire Louisiana Territory from France.

New Waves of Settlers Hit the Colonies

The North American colonies may have started out predominantly British, but they didn't stay that way for long. The colonies needed more laborers, and desperately poor European peasants needed work. After 1700, Europeans started migrating to the northern Atlantic coast in such numbers that by 1750, the white population of North America had quadrupled. These new waves of settlers not only increased the population, they changed the ethnic composition of almost every colony.

Probably the largest single group of eighteenth-century newcomers were the Scotch-Irish, a group not to be confused with either the Scotch or the Irish. The Scotch-Irish were the descendants of the Scotch Presbyterian families the British originally brought to Ireland to farm in the linen-producing regions. Although they were Protestants living in a devoutly Catholic country, religious discontent was not the main reason so many Scotch-Irish moved to North America. They left because they hated the Irish land system with its absentee

Although there were many farmers and traders in the middle colonies (New York, New Jersey, Delaware, and Pennsylvania), there were also a large number of artisans, including blacksmiths, cabinet makers, and this clock designer, who brought their much-needed skills to the region.

One of the most despised and persecuted religious sects in England in the mid-1600s were the Quakers. This satirical woodcut of a typical Quaker colony tried to show that Quaker ideas of equality were so extreme that they even included the then-outrageous idea that women were intelligent, capable, and entitled to an equal voice in the community.

landlords, high rents, and short leases. It got so bad they could never be sure from one month to the next if they would have homes or jobs, especially when they had to compete with local Irish families who were even more poor and desperate and therefore more willing to endure higher rents and a lower standard of living. Not particularly welcome in the New England area, most Scotch-Irish immigrants settled in Pennsylvania, Virginia, or the back country of the Carolinas — wherever land was less expensive and religious tolerance higher.

A relatively small number of Scotch settlers also came to the United States in the 1700s, but they were not part of the Scotch-Irish peasant migrations. The Scotch were mostly merchants, artisans, and weavers (with some farmers and laborers) fleeing Scotland's high rents and trade depression. Most settled in what is today upstate New York.

Greatly outnumbering the Scotch immigrants were the Germans, who came from an amazing number of tiny, independent German and Swiss states. They, too, had many persecuted religious sects (such as the Morovians) who sought refuge in North America, although most were Lutherans or members of the German Reformed Church who immigrated for economic rather than religious reasons — merchants and entrepreneurs who eventually established successful businesses in their new homeland. Many of these early German and Swiss immigrants settled in the Pennsylvania area, primarily because of the welcome religious tolerance of the Religious Society of Friends, known as the Quakers. The Quakers were a deeply religious Christian sect that believed in equality and in living in peace with their neighbors. In 1681, a large group of Quakers led by William Penn founded a colony along the banks of the Delaware River, calling their settlement *Philadelphia,* which is Greek for "brotherly love."

In the century following the first arrival of Sephardic Jewish colonists at New Amsterdam in 1654 (Jews originally from Spain and Portugal who fled to Amsterdam because of religious persecution), Jewish communities began to spring up in a number of other seaport towns, especially Philadelphia, Newport, and Charleston. By the time of the Revolution, over two thousand Jewish merchants and traders who had fled religious persecution in Europe were living in British colonies, enjoying more political and religious freedom than they had experienced anywhere else in the world.

The lure of America as a haven to these and other European groups stands in somber contrast to the plight of those who were brought to America against their wishes. Within a generation of the arrival of the first shipload of Africans in Virginia in 1619, Blacks, most of them slaves, could be found in almost every colony. In the course of the eighteenth century, as many as two hundred thousand Africans were brought to America as slaves, nine-tenths of them to the southern plantation colonies.

A New Haven for Immigrants

The first U.S. census in 1790 showed that nearly 1 million African-Americans and 4 million European-Americans were living in the newly independent nation. People who arrived after this date were no longer "colonists" but "immigrants" seeking an existing nation to make their permanent home. For the next two centuries, people would immigrate to the United States in staggering numbers from all over the world. The United States did not start recording immigration statistics until 1820, but figures after that date show that the stream of immigrants was continuous from 1820 to 1924 — with only occasional interruptions caused by wars and depressions.

The history of U.S. immigration can be divided up into three major waves. The first wave lasted from 1820 to 1890, during which 15 million immigrants arrived in the United States from Northern and Western Europe. The second wave took place between 1890 and 1924, when another 15 million European immigrants arrived — this group, however, was mostly from Eastern and Southern Europe and included Poles, Russian Jews, Ukrainians, Slovaks, Croatians, Slovenes, Hungarians, Romanians, Italians, and Greeks. (Large numbers of Chinese and Japanese immigrants also arrived during these periods.) The third wave occurred during the period between the end of World War II and the present. This group included European war refugees, large numbers of Southeast Asians, and a tremendous influx of people from other countries in the Western Hemisphere like Mexico, Cuba, Haiti, Nicaragua, Colombia, and Panama. A large number of Puerto Ricans migrated during this period as well, from their island homeland to cities on the U.S. mainland.

The following chapters will show why these groups came to the United States, how they made the passage, how difficult it was to adjust to their new homeland, and why they stayed — if indeed they did. As we know, not all came to the United States willingly. Some came as slaves; others came as desperate refugees from war, famine, or natural disaster. Not all realized their expectations. The streets were not paved with gold as many had believed, nor were men and women of all colors and creeds given equal respect and opportunity. Almost all still had to fight for that equality once they arrived. But regardless of their color, religion, economic status, or political ideologies, every group of immigrants that arrived in the United States made tremendous cultural contributions in every field of human endeavor from the arts to medicine, science, education, politics, and technology. They have, with their skills, intelligence, and spirits, quite literally formed the country that exists today.

Despite the oppression, discrimination, and other hardships they have had to endure, African-Americans have made outstanding contributions to U.S. culture in medicine, law, education, business, literature, music, and sports. Recent immigrants, like these shown here, have come to this country to further their education and careers.

CHAPTER TWO

African-Americans

There is always a waiting list to get into Mankelolo Ntokozo's college economics class, and it is not just because she is an enthusiastic professor who knows how to make an often dry subject come alive. An African political refugee educated in the United States, Ntokozo encourages her students to question how U.S. economic and political policies affect the rest of the world, invariably stirring up intense debates that continue long after her class period is over. A tall woman elegantly dressed in a traditional South African dashiki, Professor Ntokozo conducts her class with calm good humor and almost flawless English. (Her slight accent is from New Jersey, not South Africa.) Although she takes obvious pride in her African roots, Ntokozo is a passionately patriotic American who frequently shares her South African experiences to help her students appreciate the freedom and opportunity they enjoy as U.S. citizens. "If you have never lived somewhere else," she often says, "you cannot know how much freedom you have here."

Seventeen years ago, Mankelolo Ntokozo and her husband were each placed in solitary confinement for twenty-one days in South Africa's Moletsane police station, falsely accused of terrorism. She was eventually set free, but her husband was never heard from again. Outraged, Ntokozo joined the anti-apartheid movement and by 1980 was again arrested for terrorism against the state. This time she escaped. She had no choice but to leave her two-year-old son, Ratijawe, with her mother and flee to Botswana. From there, it took another year before she could afford to come to the United States and another three once she got here to be granted political asylum.

As with so many other immigrants to the United States, Ntokozo believed that the key to prosperity was education. Since her arrival, she has earned a bachelor's degree, two master's degrees, and a doctorate of theology — all paid for through scholarships and her own hard work. Her academic credentials and dedication to helping others have won her two soul-satisfying careers — as a professor of economics and as an assistant minister at an African Methodist Episcopal church in New York City.

While she inspires both students and congregation members with her compassion and ideals, some of her inspiration is focused a bit closer to home. Five years ago, after her mother died, Ntokozo finally succeeded in getting her son a visa to the United States. At nineteen, Ratijawe is already following in his mother's footsteps and will soon graduate with a pre-law degree — and ambitions for an active political career.

Among the First Explorers

The first Africans to arrive in North America were important members of Spanish and Portuguese expeditions during their early exploration of the Americas. Pedro Alonzo Niño, for example, was a free man and the navigator of the flagship on which Christopher Columbus sailed to the West Indies. He is generally believed to be the first African to see the Americas. When Balboa became the first European to reach the Pacific Ocean in 1513, there were thirty Black men in his party who helped him clear the first road across the isthmus (in present-day Panama) that separated the Atlantic and the Pacific oceans. Africans were with Hernando Cortés when he conquered Mexico. And in 1528, two Spanish soldiers — Alvar Núñez Cabeza de Vaca and his Black companion, an African slave named Estevánico — survived a shipwreck off the coast of Texas and were the first known non-Indians to happen upon the area that is today Arizona and New Mexico. In the sixteenth century, many of these first African voyagers stayed in the Americas, some settling in the Mississippi Valley and in the areas that became South Carolina and New Mexico.

Most Africans, however, who arrived in the Americas between the seventeenth and early nineteenth centuries were far from willing immigrants. Some came as indentured servants, most as slaves, and all but a few spent the rest of their lives in bondage, as did generations of their children.

The first twenty Africans arrived in Jamestown in 1619 when the captain of a Dutch trading vessel, the *Jesus of Lubeck*, traded them for fresh provisions. While Africans were already being imported into the West Indies as slave labor, these twenty Africans were the first Black laborers brought into British American territory. They bore Spanish names and had been baptized as Christians by their Spanish captors before the Dutch captain had kidnapped them — either

Both the rum trade and sugar plantations, like the one shown here, put the West Indies squarely in the middle of the deadly "triangular" slave trade between Europe, Africa, and the Americas. Although the first Africans brought to the West Indies to work the plantations were supposed to be indentured servants, not slaves, very few were set free after a set number of years, as these laborers were.

from a Spanish plantation or from a Spanish slave ship. (Historians are not sure which.) At that time, Christian Africans from Spanish or Portuguese colonies in the Caribbean were able to settle in English colonies with the status of indentured servant (as opposed to slave status) if they could prove they had been converted to Christianity. After their period of indenture, most of these African immigrants eventually became free men.

Africa's Slave Coast

Most of the slaves traded to American colonists came from an area in western Africa called the Slave Coast, an area that includes the present-day countries of Angola, Gambia, the Gold Coast, Guinea, and Senegal. Africans were procured as slaves along the Slave Coast in a number of ways. Some were stalked and captured personally by European slavers. At first, many were prisoners seized in intertribal battles. European traders negotiated with local African chieftains, paying them an average of about $25 a head (or the equivalent value in rum or other merchandise) for their captives — and then selling them in the Americas for about $150 a head. (After Congress declared the slave trade illegal in 1808, African slaves brought even higher prices from southern plantation owners in the United States for black-market traders willing to take the risk.)

But by the middle of the seventeenth century, a third way of procuring slaves had become more prevalent: Larger, more powerful African tribes started waging war on smaller nations for the sole purpose of taking slaves they could later sell to the Europeans. Before this time, tribal captives were treated much differently. Although forced to work for their captors, prisoners taken captive in intertribal battles were treated as human beings, not as property. Families were allowed to stay together, and some prisoners were even permitted to own property. Later, when African kingdoms waged war strictly for the purpose of taking slaves, their captives faced much harsher conditions. Many were captured in the interior and forced to make the long march to the sea in chains. When they arrived on the coast, starved and terrified, the healthy were separated from the old and sick, then branded and crammed into barracks until a slave ship arrived to take them to the Americas. Their conditions rapidly deteriorated from bad to worse to terrible. Still chained, they were crowded into the holds of slave ships for the dreaded Middle Passage across the Atlantic Ocean, usually to the West Indies, where the life that awaited them was not much better.

The Dreaded Middle Passage

The sea route slave ships followed across the Atlantic from Africa's Gulf of Guinea to ports in New England, the plantation South, or the West Indies became known as the Middle Passage. While every crossing by ship over the Atlantic was considered uncomfortable and dangerous at that time, the peril and suffering endured by African slaves was unspeakable. Two-hundred-ton sailing

The rich heritage of African culture

Along the coast of West Africa were the major kingdoms of Oyo, Ashanti, Benin, Dahomey, and the Congo. Further inland were the empires of Ghana, Mali, and Songhai, as well as the Hausa states and the states of Kanem-Bornu. Many of these were highly developed cultures with advanced social, religious, and political organizations, cultures rich in art, music, and dance. Cities like Djenne and Timbuktu grew wealthy from the area's successful cattle herding and grain agriculture, and as the cities grew, merchants began trading with Arab countries around the Mediterranean in goods such as leather, ivory, gold, animal skins, feathers, timber, and metal artwork.

vessels generally carried between four and five hundred slaves in addition to the crew and several weeks' worth of provisions. This meant that slaves had to be wedged into the holds so tightly that they could barely move at all. Additional platforms were erected between decks to use every square inch of space, often leaving only two and one-half feet between one row of people chained and lying on their backs and the platform directly above them.

The food the African men, women, and children received was usually spoiled and the water stagnant, if not actually contaminated. Their quarters had no sanitary facilities or air circulation and as a result stank with filth. On some ships, slaves were actually allowed up on a deck for a few moments of fresh air every day or so — if they were lucky.

Conditions were so horrible that many slaves chose to commit suicide by jumping overboard (or by swallowing their own tongues). Those who rebelled were shot down in cold blood or beaten to death by the crew. And some captains were not above simply tossing their cargo overboard if it suited their convenience.

Those who survived the seasickness and disgusting, cramped quarters (and one in five did not) had no idea what awaited them when they reached American ports. Whenever a slave ship was due, its arrival was announced by the town crier or by an advertisement in a local newspaper. Then householders, plantation owners, and slave dealers all gathered at the dock to meet the ship and bid against each other as the cargo was auctioned off. Slave families who had somehow managed to stay together during the crossing were now ripped apart and sold away from each other, never to meet again. They soon learned that what awaited them was a lifetime of backbreaking work without pay, meager food, and the lash of the whip. Even those who found fellow Africans employed as slaves in their new homes were often from different parts of Africa and therefore could not understand each other's language.

By the middle of the sixteenth century, more than ten thousand Africans a year were being shipped to the West Indies, where the demand and the ability to pay were the greatest. But by the seventeenth century, the slave trade was booming in the English colonies as well. Nine-tenths of the African slaves sold in the English colonies were sold to southern plantation owners.

Slavery Grows in the British Colonies

At first, English colonists preferred to use white indentured workers to help build the new colonies, laborers who agreed to work for a set amount of time (usually between four and seven years) for the employer who paid for their passage from Europe. Colonists had to work in close proximity to each other to survive and therefore preferred servants and laborers with the same language, religion, and cultural background. Blacks were their last choice; even Irish Catholic, German Protestant, and Sephardic Jewish servants were preferable. The number of indentured workers, however, was not nearly enough for the tremendous amount of work involved in establishing new settlements, and since most of the local Indians refused to work for the colonists, English colonists turned to African labor.

At first, the Dutch and French dominated the trading of slaves in the Americas, but in 1672, the King of England chartered the Royal African Company, and the English soon took control. Slave dealers made so much money transporting African slaves that they referred to their human cargo as "black gold."

The main reason more slaves ended up in the southern plantation colonies was climate. Because of the bitter winters and stony soil, New England had no large farms producing cash crops like cotton and tobacco. Farms were small and owners could not, for the most part, afford Black slaves to help with the work. The southern colonies, on the other hand, had rich soil and a warm climate, both of which were ideal for huge cotton and tobacco plantations. By the end of the seventeenth century, the plantation system was thriving in South Carolina, Virginia, Maryland, and Georgia, creating a growing demand for labor. The few southerners who could afford to own land tended to be well-educated gentlemen of leisure who passed along the job of managing and disciplining their labor force to the poor, uneducated white men they employed as overseers.

At first, plantation owners imported African laborers from the West Indies, but by the late 1700s, slave ships were sailing directly from Africa into North American ports on a regular basis. When plantation owners in Virginia wanted to keep their Black indentured servants beyond the original period of indenture, the colony made Black slavery legal with a series of laws it passed between 1660 and 1682. In 1682, the Virginia legislature passed a law stating that all "non-Christian nationalities" coming into Virginia (whether by land or by sea and whether or not they had converted to Christianity since leaving their homelands) were servants for life. By 1750, all the other English colonies had made slavery legal as well. Colonists also found it easy to rationalize the barbaric practice of slavery with the mistaken belief that Africans were an inferior race with a primitive, heathen culture.

Although New England did not import nearly the number of slaves who were imported to work on southern plantations, this region still played a major part in keeping the slave trade alive. West Indian plantations sold their molasses crop to rum distillers in New England, who in turn used the rum to buy more African slaves to sell in Barbados. Everyone profited from this "triangular trade" — everyone, that is, except the African slaves.

Within a generation of the arrival of the first shipload of Africans in Virginia in 1619, Blacks could be found in almost every colony. In the eighteenth century alone, as many as seven hundred thousand Africans were abducted and crammed onto slave ships bound for the Americas, with two hundred thousand of them coming ashore in the area between Maine and Georgia. By the time of the American Revolution, the increasingly profitable slave trade had expanded into a monstrous institution condoned and regulated by most of the supposedly "civilized" nations of the world. Over five hundred thousand Blacks were living in the colonies at the time, most of them slaves. At the same time that the ideas of freedom and equality were stirring up thoughts of revolution in American colonists, the roots of American slavery were growing deeper and deeper.

The roots of soul food

Many of the most delicious foods traditional to southern U.S. cooking were brought as provisions from Africa on the same ships used to transport African slaves — foods like yams, millet, sorghum, rice, peanuts, plantains, citrus fruits, cassava, okra, sesame seeds, black-eyed peas, greens, melegueta pepper, and palm oil. As the slaves settled into their new lands, still yearning for their African homeland, they continued to secretly practice many of their ancient beliefs and traditions, including music, dance, and the preparation of traditional foods. One of these foods was a dish from the southeast coast of Ghana known as *foufou* or *fufu*: boiled white yams pounded smooth by sticks, then rolled and dipped into a groundnut stew. Africans taken from Guinea, Nigeria, Ghana, and other West African regions where the cultivation of rice was common developed the technique of rice cookery later used by Cubans, Haitians, Puerto Ricans, and southerners in the United States to create spicy rice and bean dishes. Another rice dish called Limping Susan (made with okra) has its roots in African cooking. Even the eggplant (also widely known as guinea squash) is African and was being used in southern kitchens years before Thomas Jefferson supposedly brought it to the United States. Fresh black-eyed peas are used to prepare Hoppin' John, a dish similar to Senegal's *Thiebou Niebe*. Africans also gave Americans many words for food, like *gumbo*, the Bantu word for okra. The word *okra* itself is an African word. In West African Akan dialect it means "the soul," a probable reason traditional African-American cuisine is often called "soul food." Yams get their name from the Senegalese word *nyami*, which means "to eat," and "goobers," a southern term for peanuts, comes from the West African word *gooba*.

Not all colonists condoned slavery, however. Even before the Revolution, conscientious Quakers like John Woolman openly advocated the abolition of slavery. As they fought for their own freedom against England, more Americans began to realize that one could not believe in human freedom and at the same time live in a society where people owned other people. But before 1820, even the few Americans who openly despised the idea of slavery believed their new country would be thrown into economic turmoil if slaves were suddenly freed. Those who helped draft the new Constitution were able at least to eventually put a legal end to the trading of slaves. The Constitution stipulated that the slave trade would officially end in 1808, twenty years after it was written.

Illegal cargoes of slaves continued to slip into southern ports after that, however, and it is estimated that over fifty-four thousand "illegal" slaves entered the United States between 1808 and 1860. It would also take another fifty-five years after Congress outlawed the slave trade for Africans already in the United States to be emancipated (and well into the twentieth century before African-Americans would start to achieve full equality in U.S. society). Despite continuing prejudice, discrimination, and persecution at the hands of groups like the Ku Klux Klan, Black Americans have made outstanding contributions to every phase of U.S. life, from the arts and sciences to politics, education, religion, and sports.

Twentieth-century African Immigrants

Today, twenty-two of the thirty-six poorest countries in the world are African. In spite of decades of efforts to develop industry and agriculture, economic conditions in most of these countries continue to deteriorate as population, famine, poverty, and unemployment all continue to grow — at alarming rates. In addition, many of Africa's most educated and talented people (highly-trained African professionals and experienced businesspeople often educated at state expense) have left their homelands in the last forty years for more prosperous industrial nations such as the United States. Many analysts refer to this phenomenon as Africa's "brain drain."

The reasons these talented people continue to emigrate are strong ones. Africa's political and economic crises reached a peak in the late 1970s, when severe droughts and escalating oil prices crippled African economies. There was little or no government money left for research, education, and social services. Africa also experienced so many violent military takeovers during this period that over 60 percent of African governments became military dictatorships. As economic conditions became more desperate, civil wars, guerrilla actions, and attempted military takeovers became more common. In many cases, tribal groups fought bloody wars with each other for control. Many of the Africans who came to the United States were fleeing not only the terrible economic conditions, but political oppression and often persecution as well. Others came to the United States because it was the only way they could further their educations.

About 90 percent of the African immigrants currently living in the United States maintain close ties with family and friends back home and say they intend to return to their homelands eventually. They send money home to help support their families and community causes, and they return frequently to visit relatives and friends. Those who do eventually move back to Africa do so because of strong family ties, a desire to use their education, talent, and skills to help the development of their countries, and to break the isolation many have felt living in the United States. For many, an even more important reason is that they want to raise their children in Africa — in an environment free of drugs, crime, and racism.

African immigrants who make the decision to stay in the United States have just as strong reasons for staying. Many have professional positions that pay well, offer them opportunity for continued development, and provide them recognition for their talents. Many want the better standard of living and educational opportunities for their children the United States offers. Personal freedom and U.S. civil liberties are another strong factor, and many who stay have the added incentive of an American spouse.

African-Americans take great pride in the rich diversity of the African cultures that make up their heritage and the many ways U.S. culture has been enriched by the food, music, spirituality, art, and other folk traditions their ancestors brought with them as slaves.

When Ellis Island was restored as part of the Statue of Liberty centennial celebration in 1986, 101-year-old Margarethe Tiedmann made sure she was there to help celebrate. A scared 18-year-old immigrant getting off a ship from Bremen, Germany, she had been one of the thousands who were processed here in 1903.

CHAPTER THREE

The First Great Wave: Northern and Western Europe

Rudi Heilmann held a stein under the barrel's tap, poured his friend Albert a cold, foamy beer, and then sat down opposite him at the worn wooden picnic table. They glanced out at the beach for a moment where their children were splashing noisily with other club members. He would miss Carl Schurz Park and the camaraderie of the *Naturverein*, Rudi thought, the Nature Friends who had helped him and his wife feel at home five years ago when they first moved to Milwaukee.

Familiar sounds of zither music and German singing wafted down from the clubhouse as Albert took a long pull from his stein and sighed. "I really don't see why you and Erna have to move," he said. "Harnischfeger pays well enough and the Party's counting on you to run for alderman in September."

"Al, four long years I spent apprenticing to be a pattern maker in Hamburg's shipyards. Of course we'll miss Milwaukee's *gemütlichkeit,* but Norfolk's on the coast, and its shipbuilders are looking for pattern makers. Their union's strong, too."

Rudi's seven-year-old son Helmut ran up to the table, soaking wet and shivering under his beach towel. "*Vati, darf ich . . .*"

"English," Rudi interrupted him. "Speak English."

"Ja. Okay. Father, may I have a lemonade?"

Rudi poured his son a lemonade from the pitcher on the table and continued talking to Albert. "Socialists they have in Virginia, too, you know. Und Germans."

Albert laughed. "You're right, Rudi. But not as many. And there'll be more of the kind of people who will hate you because you're a socialist and freethinker."

Rudi looked at him for a moment in silence. "Ach, bigots there are everywhere," he said. "At least in America we can say out loud what we believe without being afraid the government will persecute us. And with votes we can

change society and with truth teach our neighbors to be more tolerant."

"You'll be mayor of Norfolk before you know it," Albert laughed. Then his smile faded. "You're a good friend, Rudi," he said sadly, "and I'm going to miss you."

Germans

Many German immigrants were unemployed craftsmen like this pattern maker from Hamburg, Germany, who settled in Milwaukee because of its established, progressive German community and familiar climate.

This story about German immigrants in the early twentieth century has its roots in the second major wave of German immigration to the United States. The first and larger wave, which began in the 1820s and reached its peak in the mid-1850s, was a rural and village movement. Whole groups of Germans (sometimes families, sometimes entire German communities) emigrated to the United States together. Most were displaced farmers or unemployed craftsmen with just enough money to buy farmland or start businesses on the U.S. frontier, the area of the United States that is today the Midwest.

But while economic considerations were the reason for most German emigration, they were not the only ones. Citizens unhappy with their corrupt and tyrannical rulers were organizing revolutions all over western Europe during the nineteenth century, particularly during the 1830s and 1840s, and the second major type of German immigrants were the political refugees who had to flee their homeland when the revolutions they supported failed. One of these revolutionary groups, the Forty-eighters, consisted of about five thousand journalists, doctors, musicians, teachers, and other intellectuals who had supported the attempt to overthrow the German government in 1848. The name Forty-eighters is misleading, however, because most of these immigrants did not arrive in the United States until the early 1850s, either because they had been imprisoned or because they had spent several years living and working in England before crossing the Atlantic. Germany's loss was America's gain. Zealous German liberals like Carl Schurz, a relentless foe of slavery and public corruption, contributed greatly to U.S. politics and political reform. Many were

The Know-Nothings

The so-called "invasion" of German, Irish, and Scandinavians in the 1840s and 1850s inflamed the hatred of U.S. "nativists" who feared that these foreign hoards would outbreed, outvote, and overwhelm the "true" stock of White, Anglo-Saxon, Protestant U.S. citizens. These "WASPs" were especially concerned about the rise in Catholicism brought about by Irish immigration. This strong dislike of foreigners led to the formation in 1849 of the Order of the Star-Spangled Banner, which soon developed into the formidable American or "Know-Nothing" Party, whose official political platform in 1856 demanded that only "native-born citizens" hold government jobs.

A modest proposal

An Irish-born English writer named Jonathan Swift (the celebrated author of *Gulliver's Travels*) often used satire to draw attention to the terrible plight of the Irish. He wrote an essay in which he proposed the grotesque idea that Irish women be paid to breed babies like cattle to produce food for the English. Under his proposed plan, women would sell their extra babies (after fattening them up for the first year) to English butchers, who would then offer them as plump morsels to their more well-to-do English customers. Swift went on to point out that this plan had many advantages. First of all, the added income would improve the standard of living of Irish peasants. Killing off the "extra" babies would also effectively deal with the growing Irish population problem, and the English wouldn't have to face the nuisance of waiting around for the Irish to starve to death. Swift's plan even had the added benefit of supplying the English with quality belts, shoes, and bags that could be made from the slaughtered babies' dead skins. Although this brilliant and vivid essay effectively used satire to show the evil brutality of England's exploitation of the Irish (and the horrible way Swift believed the Irish just seemed to be letting it happen), it did not have much impact on English society and its policies toward the Irish. What is particularly horrifying is that many thought Swift's proposal was a serious one and actually approved of it!

socialists who backed the Labor movement that had spread to the United States in the mid-1860s and who helped form many of the first U.S. trade unions.

Today, German-Americans are considered the largest ethnic group in the United States. Since 1820, when immigration officials first began recording statistics, over 7 million Germans have migrated to the United States.

The Irish: Fleeing Hunger

The Catholic peasants of Ireland lived in poverty and oppression under British rule for centuries, but by the nineteenth century, their condition had become desperate. To make Irish farmland more profitable, the English landowners decided to consolidate the small plots of land rented by Irish peasants, they started evicting the families, tearing down their houses and running them off the land. The Irish had no political rights in their own country and had no way to stop this harsh treatment except by periodic uprisings that were brutally put down by English forces. Irish peasants also faced constant harassment by English Protestants for practicing Catholicism.

Then, in the 1840s, what was already a desperate situation got even worse. Disaster struck — in the form of potato blight. For millions of people, the potato was their only source of food, and without it they starved to death. The potato blight continued for five years, producing a famine so horrific and widespread that over one-third of Ireland's population was wiped out by famine-related deaths in just a few years.

Most of the British who evicted Irish peasants were not as compassionate as this soldier, shown comforting a child.

More hazards to the journey than crossing the sea

The immigrant's dangerous journey to America started long before he or she boarded a ship in Amsterdam or Liverpool. Immigrants from Switzerland, for example, first spent over a month traveling by raft, wagon, coach, and on foot on their way north to Amsterdam on the Zuider Zee. Everyone they met along the way was determined to make a profit off of them: Innkeepers and boatmen charged exorbitant rates while toll keepers set up posts along rivers and roads and demanded payment to allow immigrants to pass. But these were all amateurs compared to those who were ready to exploit them when they got to the port city. Unscrupulous passenger brokers, provision dealers, and lodging-house keepers cheated and overcharged unwary immigrants, and an army of petty criminals did their best to fleece them of whatever money they might have left. Government officials tried to control the crime but were basically powerless. Immigrants who were so cheated that they no longer could afford the fare of ocean passage often had to turn to stealing themselves just to stay alive in the city.

The only way to survive was to get out. Hundreds of thousands of desperate Irish families boarded ships in the harbors of Dublin and Liverpool not even caring where the ships would take them. Any place had to be better than what they were leaving. Almost 2 million Irish people migrated to the United States in the 1840s alone.

The same conditions that caused people to leave Ireland influenced how and where they settled in the United States when they left ship. Most had sold what few possessions they might have had to make the trip and therefore landed without money for food or a place to stay. So even though they were weak from months and years of near starvation and the grueling voyage over, they immediately had to look for work in the port cities like New York and Boston where

Many courageous Irish women, like these who arrived in Boston in 1921, immigrated to the U.S. alone, without friends or family.

they had landed, crowding into slum housing not far from the docks, where they could more easily find jobs doing hard labor.

Unlike most other ethnic groups that had migrated to the United States before them, whole families of Irish people arrived together instead of the men arriving first and then sending for their families or sweethearts to join them.

There were plenty of jobs at first (paving streets, digging city sewage systems, building railroads, digging in coal mines, working unskilled factory jobs), but few of these short-term jobs provided an adequate livelihood. For families to get by, women had to find work taking in laundry, working as maids or scrubwomen, even doing hard physical factory work. Even children had to work full-time as soon as they were old enough to find jobs.

To make matters even worse, Irish immigrants were soon resented for taking jobs away from "real" Americans who considered the Irish to be uncouth and culturally inferior. Some employers began posting signs that said "Irish need not apply," and soon Irish immigrants were so discriminated against that many could not find work at all.

Irish immigrants never abandoned their strong Catholic faith, however, often scraping up the money to build a new parish church when they could barely afford to feed their families. In addition to the moral support their religion provided them, the Irish had a strong sense of national solidarity from being repressed by the English for so many years. They also had an amazing ability to organize politically, not by gaining power through existing U.S. political organizations but by creating their own, as they had in Ireland in defiance of their English landlords. Their political organization helped Irish immigrants get elected to important community positions, which in turn helped create the social changes that allowed them to escape their urban ghettos.

A lot more than beer and sauerkraut

Everyone loves to eat, and each immigrant culture that settled in the United States made its own wonderful contributions to American cuisine. Here is a sampling of the many foods Europeans introduced to North America:

Germans: sausages, noodles, potato dumplings, frankfurters, hamburgers, liverwurst, pretzels. (John Henry Heinz started the Heinz canned food company with the motto "57 Varieties" in the 1870s.)

Dutch: waffles, crullers, hot cocoa, buckwheat pancakes, cookies, coleslaw, chocolate bars, doughnuts, and Edam, Gouda, and other terrific cheeses.

Irish: corned beef and cabbage, Irish stew, Irish soda bread, Irish coffee. (An Irishman named Frank Carney opened America's first pizza parlor in Wichita, Kansas, in 1958, igniting a pizza craze that will not quit.)

Italians: Italian bread, minestrone soup, lasagna, ravioli, broccoli, cauliflower, fennel, eggplant, zucchini, cantaloupe, bologna.

Jews: bagels, matzo ball soup, potato pancakes, halvah, hot pastrami, blintzes, challah (egg twist bread), gefilte fish.

Hungarians: apple strudel, poppy seed fillings, Hungarian goulash, prune butter.

Greeks: filo pastry, baklava, spanakopita (spinach pies), tyropita (cheese pies).

English: apple pie, bread pudding, plum pudding, fish and chips, scones.

British and Welsh Immigrants

Although over one-quarter of a million Britons arrived in the United States in the 1820s, they attracted little attention. One reason was that their language, customs, religion, political beliefs, and even appearance were closer to those of Americans than any other group of immigrants. Another was that there was no sudden, dramatic cause (like famine or persecution) for them to leave their homeland, just the pressures of overpopulation, the decrease in available farmland, and the loss of jobs due to the industrial revolution. They did not settle in any particular area once they arrived but were absorbed into the general U.S. landscape.

Discontented Welsh farmers had already started emigrating to the United States at the end of the eighteenth century because of corn crop failures and a harsh system of absentee English landlords. Settling in New York state, Pennsylvania, Ohio, and Wisconsin, these and later groups of immigrants started exclusively Welsh communities in which everyone farmed, even those who also followed other professions, such as preachers, blacksmiths, and shoemakers.

Scandinavian Immigrants

Agricultural failures were also the main reason large numbers of Swedes and Norwegians emigrated to the United States, especially between 1868 and 1873. When they heard of the Homestead Act passed by the U.S. government and its promise of free land, many Swedes and other Scandinavians started large farms in the upper midwestern states of Wisconsin and Minnesota, where the land and climate were somewhat similar to that of the homeland they had left behind. They gave their communities names like New Sweden or New Norway and retained many of their customs and traditions.

Trying to carve out a farm on what was then the western frontier was very difficult to immigrants who had never cleared a forest, built a log cabin, or put up miles of fencing. Not only was it hard, exhausting work, but frontier immigrants also had to endure devastating epidemics of fever and ague and, in the 1860s, raids by Sioux Indians who were fighting against the U.S. government to restore their tribal land.

German Jews

In 1654, a Dutch ship, the *St. Charles*, brought the first handful of Jewish settlers (who had already fled persecution in Spain and Portugal for safe refuge in Amsterdam) to the colonies. For the next two centuries, only a few Jewish immigrants arrived in North America, and American Jews remained a tiny

Under the gaze of immigration officials, three survivors of the Holocaust — the genocide directed against Jews by Nazi Germany during World War II — put the finishing touches to the *sukkah* (a bough-covered hut) they have built to celebrate the Jewish holiday Succoth. They have been temporarily detained on Ellis Island, New York, on their way into the United States.

minority. That changed radically in 1830, when German Jews emigrated to the United States in larger numbers, along with — and for basically the same economic and political reasons as — most other German immigrants. Between 1830 and 1880, over one-quarter of a million German Jews entered the United States. They settled not only in large cities along the Atlantic seaboard, but in towns and cities throughout the Midwest, South, and the Far West as well.

German Jews involved themselves in all types of business activity in the United States, often starting small as poor peddlers, tailors, or shopkeepers and working their way up to become highly successful business owners and bankers. Many pursued a higher education in the United States to become doctors, lawyers, and other professional people. Even the most poor quickly moved up into the U.S. middle class.

German Jewish immigrants clung to their religion in the United States, but in their eagerness to become Americanized, they changed some of its orthodox customs and traditions to adapt to their new surroundings. They added sermons and choirs, had Hebrew prayers translated into English, and instead of keeping women in separate, curtained areas during services, established pews where families could sit and worship together. These changes were the base upon which the movement known as Reform Judaism was built.

By 1880, German Jewish immigrants were well assimilated into the middle class and felt they had very little in common with the waves of poor and persecuted Eastern European Jews who arrived after 1880. Like other Jews throughout Western history, however, Jewish German-Americans were to learn that simply being Jewish would be enough to set them apart from the non-Jewish world. And this simple fact would be enough to lead them to their common identity with the Jews of Eastern Europe.

Prejudice and stereotypes

Ethnic stereotypes run the gamut from silly to malicious, but even the supposedly harmless ones can hurt. No one wants to be reduced to the level of a two-dimensional cartoon. Common stereotypes include the notions that all Italians are connected with organized crime, all Scandinavians are sexually uninhibited, all Russians are godless communists, all Germans are humorless and strict disciplinarians, all Scots are cheap penny pinchers, all Irish are alcoholics, all Jews are greedy, all English are stuffy prudes, and all French are hot lovers.

By 1900, hundreds of thousands of Jews and other Eastern European immigrants lived in an area on the Lower East Side of Manhattan no larger than a square mile. In spite of the poverty and dismal tenements, its streets pulsated with life and energy.

CHAPTER FOUR

The Second Great Wave: Southern and Eastern Europe

As he helped his Dad wait on the exasperating old women who seemed to take hours making up their minds whether to buy suit cloth from the brown bolt or the black one, twelve-year-old Sam Goldfadden longed for Tuesday afternoon to finally end. It was theater night on Hester Street, and the Yiddish Theater was presenting one of Jacob Gordin's Yiddish comedies. His whole family was going to attend, even his youngest sister, four-year-old Rachel.

Sam appreciated what a treat this was. He knew how hard his parents worked just to pay their two-dollar-per-week rent. His Dad worked at his store twelve hours a day while his mother stitched blouses on an old sewing machine in their cramped apartment living room. She worked from dawn sometimes to nine or ten o'clock at night, stopping only long enough to shop, cook their kosher meals, and care for little Rachel. The theater was their one luxury.

Everyone in the neighborhood went to the Yiddish theater — sweatshop workers, rabbis, housewives, shopkeepers, scholars. Whether a silly farce or a serious melodrama, the plays that writers like Jacob Gordin presented had a ring of truth because they were based on the everyday life of Jewish immigrants in the ghetto, on the lives of families just like his own.

Finally, it was time to lock up the store and head home. As always, the street was crowded with a throng of pushcart peddlers, carriages, and people hurrying home after a long day at work. Sam thought about how much he loved New York. The Lower East Side pulsated with life and energy, bursting with a rich cultural life. Coffee houses (or "coffee and cake parlors," as they were called) were filled with an incredible variety of people ranging from Hebrew scholars engrossed in the study of ancient language and literature, to revolutionaries, poets, writers, actors, and musicians. Sam could not wait to grow up and be part of it. And tonight his worn and tired parents would watch the play

Too dark, too strange

Until the 1880s, most European immigrants to the United States had been fair-skinned Anglo-Saxon and Teutonic types, either Protestant or Catholic, with a fairly low rate of illiteracy and a familiarity with constitutional government. Many of the Southern and Eastern European immigrants who arrived after 1880, by comparison, had darker hair and complexions, radically different religious traditions, a high rate of illiteracy, and little experience with the workings of constitutional government, qualities that some Americans believed made them too strange, too foreign — in some cases, too evil — to ever assimilate into U.S. society.

and laugh and feel young again. Sam, practically bursting with excitement, raced ahead to beat his Dad to their front door.

The Second Wave

Unlike the immigrants from Northern and Western Europe, few of the immigrants that made up the second great wave (those from Southern and Eastern Europe) became farmers. Like young Sam Goldfadden's parents, almost all settled in larger U.S. cities. Like earlier immigrants, these Jews, Russians, Italians, Serbs, Croats, Poles, Romanians, Greeks, and other immigrants from Southern and Eastern Europe relied on letters from relatives and neighbors who had already emigrated, and they tended to seek out the communities where these friends and relatives lived.

Eastern European Jews

Polish Jews escaping Russian persecution in the early 1920s wait in a quarantine station in the port city of Danzig. The sign is written in Yiddish and uses both Hebrew and Roman characters to tell where to get the necessary paperwork to emigrate on the next ship sailing for the U.S.

The Jews of Eastern Europe began to leave their homes in great numbers in 1881 when anti-Semitism set off waves of bloody anti-Jewish riots. The government of the Russian Czar had forced most Jews to live in an area of southern Russia called the Pale of Settlement. Here they were restricted to poor, small towns called *shtetls*. They were also restricted to certain occupations and forbidden to own land, and their children were denied education. Jewish families were attacked and murdered without provocation by peasant mobs who then mutilated their bodies and destroyed their property. To make matters worse, in the early 1880s the Russian government suddenly expelled over twenty thousand Jews from the cities of Kiev, Petersburg, and Moscow.

Ellis Island

Twelve million of the sixteen million immigrants who entered New York Harbor between 1892 and 1954 passed through what came to be known as the "Isle of Tears" — Ellis Island.

Because there were so many people being processed at once, the experience often seemed scary and overwhelming. Disembarking ship passengers were ushered into an enormous room where doctors examined them one at a time (for about six seconds each), then wrote a single chalk mark on their clothing. Those who were chalked with a symbol — such as E, H, Pg, X or X with a circle around it — would then be pulled from line and held for further examination. The doctors were marking people who had physical abnormalities or potentially contagious diseases. An E was for eye diseases, H for heart problems, Pg for pregnancy, X for mental retardation, and X with a circle around it for insanity — all conditions that meant the person could be denied entrance into the United States. Actually, fewer than 2 percent were denied, however, unless their conditions were contagious or

they required care and had no one in the United States who could help them. Even these were usually housed and treated in hospitals on the island and then allowed to enter the country.

Next, the immigrants were lined up in front of inspectors' desks for questioning. If an immigrant's name was misspelled on the ship's passenger list or the examiner simply could not pronounce it (which happened often), he assigned the immigrant a new version, which became the person's legal American name.

Then came more questions: "How much money do you have?" "Do you have a job in America?" "Do you have a place to stay?" These were tricky questions, because if a person had less than twenty-five dollars or no definite job prospects or place to stay he or she could be turned back. For those who survived the inspections and interrogations, however, the "isle of tears" became the joyous gateway to a world of exciting opportunities their newly adopted land had to offer.

Although most Eastern European Jews had not been farmers, their livelihood as traders and peddlers depended on those who were, and when the farmers were displaced by greedy landowners (as they had been throughout most of the rest of Europe), the Jews lost their livelihoods as well.

Weary Eastern European immigrants wait in the Great Hall of Ellis Island to be processed for admittance to the U.S. Once a picnic ground for the early Dutch settlers, Ellis Island is a small island off the southwest coast of Manhattan that served as the country's main immigration station from 1891 to 1954. At the height of its activity, the Ellis Island station could process 1 million people a year.

These new groups of Jewish immigrants differed from the earlier wave of German Jews in a number of important ways. First of all, because they had been forced to live apart from non-Jews, they did not become assimilated into the cultures of their Eastern European homelands the way German Jews had. Instead, they preserved their own distinct language (Yiddish) and their own customs and religious traditions. Almost all Eastern European Jews were also intensely religious and clung more strongly to the traditions of their religion than German Jews. Most lived by rules that governed when and where they worshiped and even how they dressed.

The already well-established German Jewish immigrants with their reformed faith and middle-class, Americanized life styles were horrified at the wave of Jewish immigrants from Eastern Europe. They felt uncomfortable with these newcomers' orthodox practice of religion, their strange clothes, their radical political ideas, and what they considered to be an uncouth language mix known as Yiddish (a mixture of Hebrew, German, and various Slavic dialects). In spite of their dislike and resentment of Eastern European Jews, however, well-organized German Jewish charitable organizations did everything they possibly could to relieve the poverty and despair of the newer Jewish immigrants and to make their transition to U.S. life easier.

After 1890, about two-thirds of the United States' Jewish population was concentrated in just a handful of cities: New York, Chicago, Philadelphia, and Boston, although large groups also settled in Cleveland, Baltimore, Los Angeles, and Pittsburgh. They came from Eastern European countries like Russia, Poland, Latvia, Lithuania, and the Ukraine. The biggest Jewish population of all was in New York City, where they supplied the bulk of the labor needed by New York's garment industry.

Although they worked hard for very little money, most Eastern European Jewish immigrants were frugal, often saving enough money to start department stores (such as Gimbel's and Bamberger's), clothing manufacturing firms, book publishing houses, and newspapers. Jewish doctors like Jonas Salk and Albert Sabin, who developed cures for polio and other dreaded diseases, made outstanding contributions to medicine, while other Jewish immigrants contributed to music, the arts, and entertainment. In politics and social services, Jews (many of them socialists) worked hard to change the terrible working conditions in many U.S. industries.

Not all of their fellow countrymen appreciated either the gains or the cultural and economic contributions made by these Jewish immigrants. In fact, for many the opposite became true. In the 1890s, social clubs and societies began excluding Jews, and by the 1920s, almost every leading U.S. college and university had quotas limiting the number of Jews who could enroll during any given year. When communism began to spread in Eastern Europe after World War I, many Americans became terrified that it would take hold in the United States as well. Because Eastern European Jews had what were considered to be radical socialist leanings, they were the first to bear the brunt of the anti-communist Red Scare that started in 1919.

American hate-mongers made no distinction between Eastern European Jewish immigrants and the German Jews who had immigrated long before them, so all American Jews were targeted with anti-Semitism, a fact that drew the two groups closer together. By the time the most terrible event in all of Jewish history occurred, the murder of 6 million European Jews by the Nazis in World War II, American Jews had put aside their differences and adopted a common identity.

Ethnic communities, like this Jewish one on New York's Lower East Side around 1900, were filled with signs for goods and services in the language of the old country so everyone could read them, even the newcomers.

The Slavic Immigrants

A large number of immigrants from very different ethnic backgrounds were lumped together (often incorrectly) under the general heading of Slavs because of the common assumption that they all spoke variations of the same language. These nationalities included Great Russians, White Russians, Ukrainians, Poles, Hungarians, Romanians, Serbians, Latvians, Lithuanians, Bohemians, and Czechoslovakians (among others). Not only were most of their languages totally different from each other, so were their spiritual beliefs and social customs. The only things these immigrant groups *really* had in common with each other were the kinds of societies they left behind in Eastern Europe and the situations they encountered when they arrived in the United States.

Immigrants who came to the U.S. from rural, non-industrial areas in Eastern Europe, like these peasant women from Czechoslovakia who arrived in New York in 1939, were often ridiculed for their old-fashioned customs and ways of dressing.

Gypsy in their souls

According to 1990 census figures, the Gypsy population of the United States is somewhere between five hundred thousand and 1 million. Starting in India (Romani — their universal language — is derived from a Hindi dialect), Gypsies have experienced a series of never-ending migrations to avoid persecution, fleeing first to Persia (present-day Iran), then to Turkey and Egypt, then to the nations of Europe. The word *Gypsy* comes from a corruption of "Egypt," one of their last stopovers on their way to Europe; they prefer to call themselves "Rom."

For centuries, Europeans have stereotyped Gypsies as tambourine-playing, fortune-telling con artists who travel around the countryside in filthy caravans. When Europeans started immigrating to the United States, they brought the stereotype with them, and as a result, Gypsies are persecuted and discriminated against in the United States even today. Many states still have active anti-Gypsy laws on their books. As a result, some Gypsies tend to shun the mainstream of U.S. life and live private, secluded lives. One of the most successful Gypsies in the United States was the award-winning actor Yul Brynner.

The great majority of these Slavic immigrants were displaced peasant farmers who became industrial laborers in the United States, settling in such major industrial cities in the Northeast and Upper Midwest. Only a few became farmers. Small clusters of Czechs started farms in Iowa, Nebraska, and other areas of the Midwest. Some Russian peasants took up farming in Kansas and North Dakota, the Wends (Slavs from Lausitz, Germany) wandered into Texas, and a few Polish families raised vegetables on Long Island or tobacco in Connecticut. But the great majority of Slavic immigrants earned a livelihood in the mills and in the mines.

Even though Croats, Slovenes, and Poles were Catholic, the Serbs (like the Greeks) were Greek Orthodox, and the Bosnians were practicing Muslims, they were all considered part of one group and were expected to help each other assimilate. Many resented this type of labeling and themselves disliked the other ethnic groups who were also labeled Slavs. Some groups, like the Poles, assimilated more easily because of the strong support of Catholic Church affiliations, Polish mutual aid societies, and closely knit ethnic neighborhoods in the larger cities. Other, more isolated immigrant groups, such as those from Morovia or Bohemia, for example, had few resources to help them learn and adjust to life in industrial America.

Because Slavic immigrants came from underdeveloped countries with little industrialization or advanced technology, they often found it even harder to adjust to life in the United States than other immigrant groups. In spite of their difficulties, however, Slavic immigrants have become tremendously successful in every part of U.S. society, including science, medicine, sports, entertainment, and business.

Polish refugee children arriving in New York in 1920 are met by representatives of a Polish mutual aid society who have made arrangements for their care in New York orphanages.

Young Italian girls enjoy a gala Italian *festa* given on the terrace of the New York Public Library in 1918 to raise money for Italian soldiers and sailors blinded during World War I. Many Southern and Eastern European immigrants continued to have strong ties to their homelands, often sending money to help their political and economic struggles.

The Italian Immigrants

The Italians were another group of second-wave immigrants who settled in U.S. cities, but unlike most of the other European immigrants who arrived earlier, not all Italian immigrants came to stay. Approximately 40 percent returned to Italy to visit or because they were homesick or disliked the United States. Others returned to get married or join the army; some went home to die. Once home, many decided to return to the United States.

The basic reason Italians emigrated to the United States was poverty. By the end of the nineteenth century, Italy had become one of the most crowded countries in Europe, and because of the quality of its land and its lack of natural resources, also the poorest. As in Ireland, greedy absentee landlords (the *latifondisti*) exploited the tenant farmers (the *contadini*) with a system that kept the peasants close to starvation level.

The first Italian immigrants were mostly men who came to the United States to earn a lot of money and then return to their homeland. Many eventually stayed, sending for their wives or sweethearts and settling into the same major northeastern cities the Irish had settled into before them. Also like the Irish before them, they became a minority despised by other Americans.

Although most had been farmers back in Italy, few Italian immigrants settled on the land in the United States — mainly because they lacked the money to buy farm land and equipment. Many, however, did find seasonal work helping farmers plant and harvest crops. Of those who did become farmers themselves, many took up vine growing (for wine production) in California or fruit and cotton growing in the South.

The padrone system

The Italians had one factor going for them that the Irish did not (although it was not always exactly a positive one): the *padrone* system. The *padroni* were Italian contractors who recruited unskilled laborers in Italy, paid their fares to the United States, and then contracted them out in gangs to work in mines, build railroads, and pick crops — wherever crews were needed for hard labor. The padroni made sure the new immigrants worked, and they acted as interpreters to help them find food and a place to live.

The downside of this system was that many padroni were corrupt and exploited the very people they claimed they were helping. They often misled laborers about the dangerous and unpleasant kind of work they had been hired to do. They also deducted large commissions from laborers' wages and received huge kickbacks on the exorbitant prices inn- and shopkeepers charged new immigrants for food and lodging. Word did eventually get around back in Italy about these abuses, and by the early 1900s, the padrone system had fallen by the wayside.

Italian immigrants who were already settled in the United States formed networking groups to help out the newcomers. Catholic churches in urban Italian-American parishes sponsored social and cultural activities and offered economic support. By the early 1920s, Italian communities in larger cities like New York and Chicago had established hundreds of Italian mutual aid societies such as the Unione Siciliana and the Order of the Sons of Italy.

A vendor peddling ice on Little Italy's Mulberry Street in 1897.

Italian immigrants, along with Jews, also bore the brunt of the anti-foreign hysteria that characterized the Red Scare of 1919. In a famous court case during that period, a shoe factory worker named Nicola Sacco and a fish peddler named Bartolomeo Vanzetti were charged with the murder of the paymaster and his guard at a shoe factory in South Braintree, Massachusetts, in April of 1920. Even though the evidence against them was both inconclusive and circumstantial, it came out in the trial that both of the defendants

A portrait of Italian immigrants Nicola Sacco and Bartolomeo Vanzetti, who were executed in 1927 in spite of protests from all over the world that they had been convicted for their radical socialist political beliefs and not the crime of murder.

were Italian immigrants who had supported radical movements and avoided the draft in World War I. Both were convicted and sentenced to be executed. In spite of protests from all over the world that they were convicted for their political beliefs and not the crime of murder, their appeals were denied and they were electrocuted in August of 1927. Their deaths provoked anti-American demonstrations not just in Italy but throughout the world.

Americanization Policies

Even before the second great migration wave began in the 1880s, many Americans began to fear that immigrants (whatever their ethnic background) would destroy U.S. institutions or take away land and jobs from those already in the United States. They were especially resentful of those immigrants from Eastern and Southern Europe whose customs and beliefs were most unlike their own, and they tried to pass legislation restricting both the rights of immigrants and the number of them entering the country. Some tried to put a halt to

The Black Hand

Americans who resented immigrants often blamed them (usually unfairly) for many of the country's social problems, particularly crime. Even though official government crime statistics did not bear this out, a stereotype grew of Italian immigrants being violent criminals, especially those from Sicily. Italian immigrants often relied on family networks to help them adjust to U.S. life. Unfortunately, these strong family ties, coupled with the criminal stereotype, caused the idea to grow that all Italian immigrants were connected to a mysterious criminal organization known as the Mafia or Black Hand. In the 1920s and 1930s, the group took on gangster overtones and the idea became even more widespread through books and movies that painted increasingly vivid and melodramatic pictures of unscrupulous Italian criminals. The stereotype persists even today. While it was true that Italian immigrant communities had their share of both organized and unorganized crime, crime also existed in almost every other ethnic immigrant community and in non-immigrant urban communities as well.

immigration altogether and favored deporting those who had already arrived. Others decided a better way to deal with the immigrant "problem" was to actively help "Americanize" them.

As a result, in the decade of the first World War a formal Americanization movement developed in which both public and private agencies held classes, lectures, and mass meetings to teach immigrants English, to show them the fundamentals of hygiene and personal cleanliness, and to instruct them in U.S. history and politics. The movement became increasingly patronizing and intolerant, often ridiculing those who clung to any of their traditions, customs, or ways of dressing. The Americanizers wanted every last trace of foreign culture to be stamped out, taking their movement to such extremes that Italian families would be ostracized for still eating spaghetti.

The Americanization movement failed. The crusaders were discouraged because they no longer believed immigrants could or even should be assimilated into U.S. culture and therefore started siding with those who were demanding an end to immigration. The immigrants themselves were profoundly angered and humiliated by the experience, and many became more alienated by mainstream U.S. society than assimilated into it.

At the height of the "Americanization" movement of the early 1900s, an immigrant eating the traditional food of his homeland was often looked on as an outsider, and a dish like spaghetti, now loved by Americans of all ethnic backgrounds, might have been dismissed as the "national dish" of Italian immigrants.

Hispanic-Americans today form the fastest-growing ethnic group in the United States. This Central American woman and her family have gotten off to a good start on their new life in Brooklyn, New York.

CHAPTER FIVE

Immigrants from the Americas

ilda Garcia asked her secretary to reschedule the late afternoon board meeting and then left early to shop for a Mother's Day present. There were few days in the year more important to her, and no one was more worthy of honor than the woman who had risked all to give her children a better life.

In 1972, Hilda, her mother, four brothers, and two sisters had left behind a life of crushing poverty when they abandoned their one-room, dirt-floored home in Enseneda, Mexico, and illegally crossed the border into California. Hilda had been sixteen and scared, but grateful that at least her family was together again. Before she was twelve, she and two of her sisters had to spend several years in an orphanage because her mother just could not afford to raise all seven of her children after Hilda's father died. Now, almost twenty-five years later, Hilda and her siblings had built prosperous lives for themselves in the United States and had done it without costing California's taxpayers a penny.

Three days after her family arrived in Santa Ana, Hilda enrolled in school and immediately found an after-school job working in a neighborhood hamburger joint. Because she was the oldest and the family needed her income, she soon dropped out of school to work full time. Life for Hilda, her mother, and her six brothers and sisters was hard, but somehow they got by. They avoided the option of government support, even when Hilda's emergency appendectomy meant years of paying off hospital bills in small monthly installments.

With her mother's enthusiastic support, Hilda never stopped believing in herself or trying to improve her life. Within eight years, Hilda had worked herself up to office manager of a furniture store, a position that earned her twenty-five thousand dollars a year. When Congress passed new laws in 1986 granting amnesty to some illegal aliens, Hilda applied for and was granted permanent residence status by the U.S. government. She passed her high school equivalency exam in 1987 and immediately enrolled in evening college courses, which earned her a degree in business administration five years later.

Hilda also never stopped reaching out to others who were struggling to make it in her community. She is still active in volunteer work in a local

A U.S. immigration officer talks to Mexican refugees in 1916 at the U.S. end of the International Bridge at El Paso, Texas. Thousands of Mexican peasants crossed the U.S.-Mexican border to escape their country's desperate economic conditions after years of political revolution.

women's shelter, organizes fund raisers to support Hispanic-American political interests, and is an active member of a government committee on affirmative action. She is also a powerful role model for her own two daughters. Today, she carries a briefcase instead of a peasant's wash basket and makes over sixty thousand dollars a year as a government-funding specialist for the Southern California Training Council, an organization that provides employee training programs.

It took two hours of serious shopping, but Hilda finally found the perfect Mother's Day presents: a simple gold-cross pendant and a dozen long-stemmed roses — for the wonderful woman who never lost her faith.

Crossing the Borders

While Europe continued to be the main source of U.S. immigrants after 1880, the flow now started to include substantial numbers of Hispanic, Caucasian, and Black people from Latin American countries as well as immigrants from Canada.

Most Latin American countries finally achieved their independence in the nineteenth and early twentieth centuries but continued to suffer periods of economic instability and political tyranny long after they were free of their harsh European rulers. Ever since, citizens of these countries have come to the United States fleeing revolution, war, ruthless dictatorships, and devastating economic depressions.

Immigrants from countries in the Americas had a distinct advantage over immigrants from anywhere else in the world when it came to the numbers of people allowed to enter the United States. Congress enacted quota laws to set limits on the annual number of immigrants the United States would admit from specific foreign countries, but these laws did not apply to people living in the Western Hemisphere until 1952, when Congress passed the restrictive

McCarran-Walter Immigration Act. Even then, the new system had loopholes that favored Western Hemisphere political refugees, immigrants seeking temporary farm employment, and citizens of U.S. territories such as Puerto Rico, the Canal Zone, and the Virgin Islands.

Mexicans: The Largest Group of Latino Immigrants

Hispanic-Americans today form the fastest-growing ethnic minority in the United States. Numbering about 22.4 million in 1992, they make up the second-largest minority in the nation, after African-Americans. About 60 percent of the U.S. Latino population can trace its origins back to Mexico.

Mexican migration patterns are unique for several reasons. The first Mexican-Americans, for example, did not immigrate at all. They were living in the parts of northwestern Mexico that became U.S. territory when the 1848 Treaty of Hidalgo marked the end of the Mexican-American War. In addition to disputed parts of Texas, this area includes all or part of the present U.S. states of California, Arizona, Utah, Wyoming, Nevada, New Mexico, and Colorado. Although Mexicans began crossing into Texas to work the cotton harvests in the years after the Civil War ended in 1865, the first Mexicans to actually move to the United States came around 1900. As Mexico's postwar economy went from bad to worse, thousands of Mexican peasants crossed the U.S.-Mexican border to escape their country's desperate economic conditions. (The living conditions and discrimination they encountered in the United States, however, were often worse than those they left behind.)

In 1910, another class of Mexicans fled to the United States. These were educated and often wealthy landowners and their families who were escaping Mexico's political revolution. Most expected to return to Mexico as soon as the revolution was crushed and Mexico's political and economic conditions returned to normal. Even though the revolution was successful, some did eventually return to try to reclaim land they had owned, but most made the decision to stay and make a new life in the United States.

By the end of World War I, Mexicans were also entering the United States to work as migrant laborers on large farms in California's Central Valley and soon after that began to work their way to states farther north to harvest other crops. Many of these were only temporary migrants who returned to Mexico after each season was over. Other temporary migrants often stayed in the United States after a harvest to wait for the next season or to look for better-paying jobs. Of these, many eventually became permanent U.S. residents.

When World War II broke out in 1942 and much of the U.S. work force either enlisted in the military or took jobs in defense plants, farm workers were in such short supply that the United States negotiated a temporary wartime agreement with Mexico called the Mexican Farm Labor Supply Program (unofficially called the Bracero Program, *bracero* meaning "day laborer"). U.S. employers gained so many benefits from the program that they demanded the arrangement be continued for another twenty years after the war ended — to 1964. During that period, increasing numbers of Mexicans migrated to states as far away from Mexico as Minnesota and Wisconsin.

When World War II broke out, U.S. farm workers were in such short supply that the U.S. negotiated a temporary agreement with Mexico to bring in Mexican workers. Farmers were happy to get the help, and unemployed Mexican laborers were happy to get the work, even if it was low paying and took them away from their families for months at a time.

Puerto Rico became a possession of the United States in 1898 as a result of the Spanish-American War, and its citizens were granted U.S. citizenship in 1917.

One advantage of the Bracero Program was that even if Mexico's immigration quotas were filled, Mexican laborers could still legally enter the United States to work. They were issued special documents and were kept track of by government records. After the program ended, many "undocumented" workers kept pouring into the United States without the green cards that identified them as "legal aliens" under the new quota laws. Without documentation, aliens are subject to arrest and deportation. This fear of deportation makes them easy prey for unscrupulous employers who know they can get away with overworking and underpaying them in sweatshops, as scab labor (to replace striking union workers), and in domestic employment, because complaining to authorities could get them arrested for entering the United States illegally.

Although there are now Mexican-Americans in most parts of the United States, some areas have especially large concentrations. More than 90 percent live in or near cities. The Los Angeles area has more Mexicans than any other city in the Western Hemisphere except for Mexico City, and there are also sizable Mexican-American communities in Denver, Kansas City, Chicago, Detroit, and New York.

Puerto Ricans

Puerto Ricans enjoy a different status from other Hispanic-Americans: They are citizens of the United States by birth, whether they were born in their homeland or on the U.S. mainland, and they are free to move throughout the United States without passports or other documentation.

The first substantial wave of Puerto Ricans arrived during World War I (1914-1918), when the booming U.S. war economy produced thousands of new jobs. Some continued to arrive during the prosperous roaring twenties, but the main wave did not begin until after the end of World War II in 1945. Puerto Ricans could now travel quickly and cheaply to mainland cities by plane and are, in fact, often described as making up the first mass air migration to the United States.

Because of severe farm labor shortages, a contract labor program was started that employed twenty thousand workers annually throughout the Northeast, in an area that extended as far west as Michigan. Not all Puerto Ricans came to the United States to work on farms, however. In the postwar industrial boom, factory jobs became available in the United States that paid ten times the wages Puerto Ricans were making on the island's sugar plantations.

As U.S. citizens, Puerto Ricans did not have to pass through the usual immigration intake points that process foreigners, and they did not need passports or visas, so it was hard to keep track of the actual numbers that traveled both to and from the mainland. Large numbers of Puerto Ricans continue to travel back and forth for business reasons, education, vacations, family visits, baptisms, or funerals. Many who moved to the mainland intending to stay have decided to return to Puerto Rico, some to start businesses there, others because mainland cities did not offer the economic opportunities they had expected. Others have moved back simply because they were homesick.

While inexpensive air fare and access to a wide range of new public services (such as welfare) made the move to the U.S. mainland much easier for

A large Puerto Rican family arrives in Florida in 1946, part of the first ethnic migration to travel to the United States by plane. As U.S. citizens, Puerto Ricans did not have to pass through the usual immigration intake points, and they did not need passports or visas, so it was hard to keep track of the actual numbers that traveled both to and from the mainland.

Puerto Ricans than for foreign immigrants who arrived before them, in other ways Puerto Ricans found the move much more difficult. They arrived at a time when many of the slum tenements in large U.S. cities were being torn down and replaced by integrated public housing, so many did not have the support of closely knit ethnic neighborhoods like those that formed in the tenements of New York's East Harlem and South Bronx.

Another difference was job availability. After the mid-1950s, factory wages were beginning to decline and increased technology and automation were eliminating the unskilled jobs that had helped earlier immigrant groups get their starts.

In spite of continuing struggles against poverty and discrimination, Puerto Ricans have enriched the culture of cities throughout the United States. Members of New York's large and flourishing Puerto Rican community (who refer to themselves as "Nuyoricans") have their own Spanish-language newspapers, television and radio stations, bilingual public officials, and stores and restaurants operated by and for Spanish-speaking New Yorkers. Nuyoricans also have a thriving cultural community active in literature, theater, and the arts.

According to the 1990 census, about 2.7 million Puerto Ricans now live on the mainland, with about two-thirds residing in the New York City area (including nearby New Jersey). Chicago also has a large Puerto Rican community.

Cubans

Cuba has a history of political rebellion and exile that dates back over four centuries. After Spain conquered Cuba in 1511, it ruled the Caribbean island so harshly that its inhabitants (Indians, African slaves, mestizos, and mulattos) almost constantly waged rebellions and insurrections, although with little success. Cuba was not rid of Spanish rule until Spain gave up the island to the United States after losing the Spanish-American War in 1898. The U.S. military occupied the island until the independent Republic of Cuba was finally established in 1902.

The first large group of Cubans to immigrate to the United States consisted of separatists being persecuted by Cuba's Spanish rulers during the Ten Years War (1868 to 1878). As the drive for Cuban independence increased in the 1880s and 1890s, thousands more fled to Tampa and other Cuban exile communities in New York, Key West, and New Orleans. But politics was not the only reason Cubans poured into the United States. Thousands came for economic reasons. Between 1857 and 1865, the United States increased tariff rates by over 40 percent, a move that had a disastrous effect on the Cuban cigar industry and on the Cuban economy as a whole.

Instead of ending when Cuba finally won its independence in 1902, the need for political exile actually increased. By the beginning of the 1930s, political persecution under the tyrannical rule of Gerardo Machado became so bad that thousands more left Cuba for the United States. Between 1951 and 1959, another ten thousand Cubans arrived in the U.S., fleeing a ruthless dictator named Fulgencio Batista. This time, Miami became the most important exile community.

As bad as political and economic conditions had been up to that point, the major flow of Cuban exiles did not begin until Fidel Castro took power in 1959 and established his Soviet-backed regime. Between 1959 and 1979, over 1 million Cubans sought refuge in the United States, a number that represented over one-tenth of the entire Cuban population. While some of these exiles were poor peasants fleeing persecution for political reasons, most were wealthy or middle-class Cubans who were likely to lose their property under Castro's newly imposed and Soviet-backed communist system. Under communism, all industries were "nationalized" and became the property of the state.

In early 1980, another 125,000 Cubans fled to the United States in small boats from the Cuban port of Mariel. When the U.S. government later found that an estimated 3,000 of these refugees had serious criminal records, it jailed most of them and tried to send them back to Cuba. It took eight years of negotiation to get Castro to agree to take any of them back.

A Cuban couple and their children, still shaken from the fear and trauma of a three-day ordeal on their makeshift escape raft, are comforted by Miami Cuban-Americans who will help them get settled in their new homeland.

After the Soviet Union broke apart in 1990, bringing with it the end of Soviet aid to Castro's government, the Cuban economy quickly suffered serious shortages of nearly everything. In spite of the lack of political and economic support, however, Castro insisted on continuing with his restrictive policies, giving Cubans even more reason to seek refuge in the United States. In 1994, after thousands of Cubans fled their island on tiny rafts (with dozens

The Freedom Flights

In 1965, Fidel Castro agreed to permit Cubans with relatives in the United States to leave Cuba on specially chartered planes (unless they were young men of military age). Nearly three hundred thousand Cubans were carried to the United States on these Freedom Flights between 1965 and the end of the agreement in 1973.

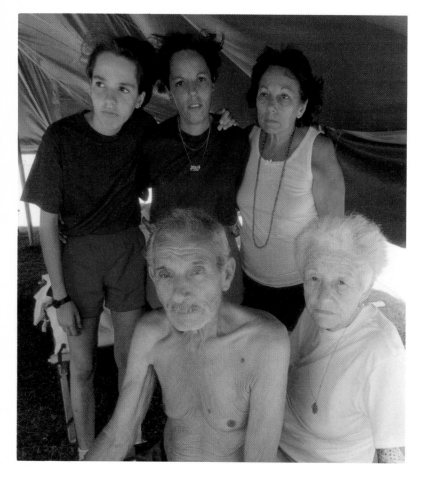

killed by dehydration, sharks, and rough seas), the two governments agreed that the United States would legally accept up to twenty thousand Cubans a year. In 1995, however, President Clinton incensed Cuban exiles by reversing that policy, announcing that refugee rafters would be returned to Cuba instead of routinely admitted to the United States as they had been in the past. For the time being, at least, this closed the doors on what had been a safe haven for Cuban refugees for thirty-five years.

Although about 60 percent of all Cuban-Americans live in Florida (with the heaviest concentration in and around Miami), many Cubans moved out of South Florida to New Jersey towns like Hackensack, Hoboken, and Union City. Chicago also has a large Cuban-American population.

A Cuban family who somehow made it safely to the U.S. base at Guantanamo Bay in 1994.

Central and South American Immigrants

In the 1960s, immigrants from Latin America began to include millions of other people from Caribbean and Central or South American countries. Salvadorans began arriving in 1976 when a devastating depression in their country was followed by the start of a civil war. Thousands of Nicaraguans and Guatemalans fled political terror for refuge in the United States throughout the late seventies. Panamanians, already familiar with U.S. culture from the long U.S. presence in the Canal Zone, moved to the United States for better economic opportunities. Immigrants from the Dominican Republic and Ecuador came in growing numbers to escape poverty and political instability. Colombia, which had already had 15 percent of its population leave the country for Venezuela, lost thousands more who headed north for the United States.

Before some Latin American economies were crippled by economic crises in the 1980s, wealthy citizens of Venezuela, Chile, Colombia, and Argentina (who saw the crash coming and were afraid they would lose their fortunes) fled to Miami. They brought such tremendous amounts of money into the city that Miami experienced an almost miraculous economic rebirth.

Little Havana

Little Havana is a four-square-mile neighborhood within the city limits of Miami where just about everything — stores, restaurants, schools, churches, theaters — exists to serve the Cuban-American and other primarily Spanish-speaking residents.

Black Migrations from the West Indies

Beginning in the early twentieth century, a stream of Black immigrants moved into New York's Harlem (and other northern cities) from the Caribbean islands of Jamaica, Barbados, Trinidad, and other parts of the British West Indies. By 1920, over one-fourth of Harlem's population was West Indian.

Like African-Americans, West Indians trace much of their ancestry to Africans who were brought to the Western Hemisphere against their will to

Waving the red and blue flag of Haitian revolution, these Haitian exiles dance for joy in the streets of Miami's "Little Haiti" in January 1986 when the U.S. State Department erroneously reported that Haitian dictator Jean-Claude Duvalier had been overthrown.

Haiti: Escape from political tyranny

Haiti's Black population finally drove out the French in 1804 and proclaimed the colony's independence, massacring almost all the remaining white inhabitants. The plantations, sugar mills, irrigation works, and roads all fell into ruins. For the next 150 years, various Black rulers tried to rebuild the ravaged country, but political revolutions continued to reduce Haiti to even worse misery. In December of 1990, a leftist Roman Catholic priest named Father Jean-Bertrand Aristide became Haiti's first democratically elected president. When he was overthrown in September of 1991, thousands of Haitians who had supported him fled for their lives to Florida in small boats, only to be sent back to Haiti by the U.S. government a few months later. While many Americans favored accepting the Haitians as immigrant refugees, others wanted their entry denied, claiming the state and federal costs to shelter and settle these families would be too great. The United States finally sent troops to Haiti in 1994 to stop the political bloodshed, reinstate Aristide as president, and ensure Haiti's peaceful transition to a democratic government.

work as slaves. But while West Indian groups share the same African ancestry of Black Americans, they consider themselves culturally different, not just from native-born African-Americans but from each other as well. Although each island was originally claimed by the Spanish and has a history of slavery, the cultures are very different because they later interacted with different European colonial powers. The language and culture of Haiti, for example, as well as Guadeloupe and Martinique (both of which are departments, akin to states, of France), have strong French influences, while those in Barbados and Jamaica have a British flavor. The French (like the Spanish) brought Roman Catholicism with them, while most of the British practiced some form of Protestantism.

Because of these cultural differences, many West Indian-Americans have found themselves becoming minority groups within a larger minority group. In spite of their differences, many West Indian-Americans like the Jamaican-born Black leader Marcus Garvey, who spent his life devoted to improving conditions for Black workers, inspired among Black people throughout the United States a sense of pride in their African heritage.

Our Canadian Neighbors

Native North American cultures have long lived on and traveled throughout the continent with little regard for state and national boundaries. European colonists, on the other hand, were quick to divide up (and fight over) the continent. Canada, for example, has been separated from the United States by the forty-ninth parallel since the European settlement of North America began, and people have been migrating back and forth across that border ever since. By 1870, about five hundred thousand Canadians had crossed the unguarded border to make their homes in the United States, and the number increased steadily until 1930, when the number of people migrating in both directions became about equal.

Boxball, anyone?

The game of basketball was invented by a Canadian immigrant named Dr. James Naismith in 1892, but if he had gotten his way, the NBA would be the National Boxball Association today. Shortly before the first basketball game was to begin at the YMCA Training School in Springfield, Massachusetts, Naismith asked the janitor to tack up two boxes on either side of the gym. The janitor could not find large enough boxes, so he substituted peach baskets instead. They worked so well that the game of "basketball" was an immediate success.

While some people had originally moved to Canada from other countries before migrating to the United States, most Canadian immigrants were native-born Canadians of either British or French descent. Almost all moved for better job opportunities.

Most British Canadians simply blended into the U.S. communities they entered, although some maintained clubs and associations with other Canadian immigrants. French Canadians (mostly from Quebec) did not assimilate quite as readily. Many were from large, devoutly Catholic farming families who found more work and better wages in New England textile mills and small factory towns than they could in Quebec. Some settled as far west as Kansas, Illinois, and Michigan. Individuals from these communities traveled back and forth across the border and continue to maintain strong cultural, religious, and even political ties to Quebec.

While many multinational U.S. corporations have large investments in Canada, there have also been many successful Canadians who have started businesses in the United States. Two of the most successful were the Ontario-born Kraft brothers, James and Charles, who founded a packaged food empire when they started their cheese-processing company in Chicago in 1904.

Cars approach the U.S.-Canadian border crossing at Blaine, Washington, on their way to the United States. Each day, thousands cross the border — in both directions — to go to work, sightsee, or visit friends.

This Japanese-American woman holds a picture that was taken of her and her husband in the early 1900s. A former "picture bride" now living in Hawaii, she did not meet her husband-to-be until the time of their wedding. Whether their dreams and expectations were fulfilled or they met with disappointment, the strength and courage of picture brides were a major reason Japanese immigrants flourished in spite of the hardships and discrimination they faced.

CHAPTER SIX

The Asians

It is ten minutes to nine, Nguyen Oanh is happy to note — almost closing time. He is tired, but selling three laser printers, an IBM 486, two CD-ROM players, and about a half-dozen modems has made it a profitable day. For the first time all evening, his computer store is almost quiet. His wife is busy at the register counting up the day's receipts, his teenage daughter is advising a last stray customer about fax software, and two of his sons, both college students, are busy repairing a faulty computer keyboard. Oanh was a math teacher in Vietnam, not a computer specialist, but when the communists took over, times became so hard, both economically and politically, that he decided his family needed to flee Vietnam. He is glad his children do not remember those terrible months. Oanh and some other married friends had pooled their money, bought a small boat, and secretly left Vietnam one night with fifty-five people aboard. Heading into stormy weather to keep from getting caught, they somehow made it safely to Singapore.

Many families who escaped Vietnam were confined to refugee camps, sometimes for years, before they were allowed to emigrate to the United States. Oanh's family was lucky. Four months after reaching Singapore, he landed in Houston with his wife and four children, sponsored by his brother, who had settled there eight years earlier. There a new challenge awaited them. Oanh realized that he had to learn English and acquire a skill to be able to hold a decent job, so even though he found accepting public help deeply humiliating, his family lived on welfare while he studied English and computer science. Then he got a job with a computer company, worked hard, and eventually saved the eight thousand dollars that helped him to open his mall computer store. Until last year, he and his wife worked seven days a week to get the business off the ground. Oanh smiles to himself. Now we're doing okay, he thinks — we can even take Sundays off!

Tremendous Cultural Diversity

As an immigrant from Vietnam, Oanh represents one of the most recent groups of Asians to come to the United States. But the history of Asian immigration is as old and varied as that of other immigrant groups. Asian-Americans trace their origins from countries located in four major areas: East Asia (Chinese, Japanese, and Koreans), Southeast Asia (Cambodians, Laotians, Thai, and Vietnamese), the Pacific Islands (Fijians, Filipinos, Guamanians, Hawaiians, and Samoans), and India (East Indians from India and neighboring Pakistan and Bangladesh). Each population group within these four areas has very different historical, linguistic, and social backgrounds. In fact, countries within the groups differ greatly as well.

The largest concentrations of Asian-Americans today are found in Hawaii; in the West Coast cities of Los Angeles, San Francisco, and San Diego, all in California; and in Seattle, Washington. Substantial populations also live in other large metropolitan areas, including Chicago, Boston, New York City, and Washington, D.C. Chinese-Americans are the most numerous, followed by Filipino-, Japanese-, East Indian-, Korean-, and Vietnamese-Americans.

Chinese-Americans

In the nineteenth century, the United States was expanding westward toward the Pacific Ocean. European colonists in Hawaii and in Central and South America were expanding their influence, too, especially in mining and the development of sugar and other crop plantations. When the African slave trade became illegal in the early 1800s, both the United States and the European colonies in Central and South America began looking toward Asia to satisfy their tremendous need for cheap labor. Some Chinese businessmen saw this as an opportunity to get rich and started recruiting (or kidnapping) penniless Chinese peasants to work in the Americas. These laborers were often referred to by racist Americans as "coolies," and the trading in human lives by the Chinese labor brokers was called the "pig trade."

The first major event to bring a sudden flood of Chinese immigrants to the United States was the California Gold Rush of 1848. By 1851, there were over twenty-five thousand Chinese in California. They did not arrive singly but in companies organized by local Chinese associations. For their help and sponsorship, the companies received half the gold each miner accumulated, terms most miners thought fair (even though they still had to repay the so-called coolie brokers for the cost of their passage). These first Chinese immigrants called their new home *Gum Sahn* (Gold Mountain). Most of them came from the same Chinese province — Kwangtung.

At first, the newly arrived Chinese were as welcome as anyone else.

San Francisco newspapers referred to them as "The Celestials" (because they were immigrants from the Celestial Kingdom, as China called itself) and called them "good citizens, deserving the respect of all." This good will did not last long. Competition for gold became fierce, and soon white prospectors resented "foreign" competition and began using violence and derision to try to drive the Chinese out of the mining camps. In addition, laws were passed imposing high monthly taxes on Chinese miners. Many quit mining to go into business for themselves. Some set up cooking and laundry businesses in the mining camps. Others moved into San Francisco, where they successfully operated carpentry, laundry, hotel, and restaurant businesses, although these, too, were soon heavily and unfairly taxed.

There were other equally humiliating legal measures aimed at the Chinese that did not just affect their livelihood. Laws made it illegal to rent rooms with less than five hundred cubic feet of space per person (which many Chinese families were forced to do). Chinese children were barred from attending public schools. And while it may not have been legal, many white-owned stores and restaurants owners refused to serve Chinese customers.

It was railroad construction that brought the next great wave of Chinese immigrants to the United States in the 1850s, particularly the transcontinental railroad that the Central Pacific was racing to build. Many Chinese also worked on the Northwest Pacific Railroad and the Southern Pacific. In spite of their slight builds, Chinese crews proved to be better and harder workers than any other groups working railroad construction, including the Irish. In spite of the reputation they earned, however, Chinese workers became the scapegoats when construction on the transcontinental railroad ended in 1869, throwing thousands of railroad laborers out of work. Unemployment was also rising throughout the country because the invention of new, labor-saving machines threw thousands more out of work. When the widespread unemployment led to the depression of 1873, frightened white Americans were only too glad to

The Great Depression of the 1930s was often harder on immigrants than on U.S.-born Americans. While the scarcity of jobs made it tough for both groups to feed their families, immigrants were often blamed for causing the depression. The small Ohio town where this woman ran a laundry business tried to send her and her four children back to China in 1934. Thanks to the efforts of some caring neighbors, a court protected their right to live in this country.

This cartoon ridicules the racist roots of anti-Chinese sentiment in the 1870s.

blame their troubles on the sixty-three thousand Chinese, most on the West Coast, who by 1870 were living in the United States.

By that time, the acceptance and often even friendliness that Chinese immigrants had encountered in the United States had long since been replaced by ugly racism, resentment, and violence. West Coast whites were afraid they would lose their jobs to Chinese laborers who were willing to work for less, so they formed an organization called the Workingmen's Party, whose campaign slogan was "The Chinese Must Go."

Californians soon passed laws prohibiting the Chinese from owning property or securing business licenses and even barring them from many occupations. But anti-Chinese sentiment was not just confined to the West Coast. Many Chinese immigrants had settled throughout the country in cities along the railroad routes they had helped build. Others had moved to find agricultural work. Wherever they migrated, whites resented them for the same reason: the competition for jobs.

By 1882, nationwide hatred and resentment of the Chinese had become so strong that Congress passed the first of the Chinese Exclusion Acts to halt almost all further immigration. After that, only a few teachers, businesspeople, and professionals were allowed to immigrate.

When Congress finally liberalized U.S. immigration laws in 1965, a new wave of Chinese immigrants arrived, mainly from Hong Kong. By 1980, the Chinese-American population numbered more than eight hundred thousand, of which one-third were born in the United States. But in the decade from 1980 to 1990, the Chinese-American population more than doubled to about 1.6 million. The flood of new immigrants has created problems of economic survival, overcrowding, and family tensions, but at the same time it has revitalized Chinatowns across the nation. Today, Chinese-Americans are a vital force in U.S. urban life. Many are well educated and have found employment in professional and technical fields.

Japanese-Americans

The Japanese formed the second wave of immigrants from East Asia beginning in the late 1880s, and in many ways, their experience paralleled what the Chinese immigrants had gone through before them.

When Congress passed the Chinese Exclusion Act in 1882 to stop Chinese immigration, the United States still had a great need for cheap labor and so turned instead to Japan. Some

Chinatowns

Chinatowns were more than ethnic neighborhoods. They were networks of mutual support systems that allowed Chinese-Americans to educate their children in their own language, publish and read their own newspapers, and even attend their own operas. Wherever possible, they made their living working with and selling to each other. Groups of merchants organized their own banks by putting money into a pool from which anyone could borrow. They ran their own employment agencies, rooming houses, stores, bakeries, and restaurants, and these businesses posted their signs only in Chinese. Whites rarely ventured into Chinatown neighborhoods.

Japanese immigrants were brought to Hawaii on three-year labor contracts to work the sugar plantations. Some immigrated to California with the intention of becoming farmers or working on the railroads. By 1930, the number of Japanese-Americans had increased to 140,000.

Like the Chinese before them, Japanese immigrants were initially welcomed by employers because they were healthy, hard-working males. They, too, worked in railroad construction, lumbering, and fishing and later moved into service trades and small businesses. Also like the Chinese, the Japanese soon angered many white Americans with their hard work and success, and they were soon the victims of prejudice and discrimination.

Almost all the stereotypes whites once reserved for the hated Chinese now applied to the Japanese as well: "Japs," who as Asians were also called "the Yellow Peril," were considered sly and greedy with dishonest personal habits and weird, suspicious lifestyles. The only real difference white Americans now saw between the Chinese and Japanese was that the Japanese were land hungry and did not seem as humble or as ready to put up with racist violence and prejudice, traits that supposedly made them even more dangerous than the Chinese.

In response to hostility and discrimination, the Japanese, like the Chinese, found protection and mutual support in "Little Tokyos," urban ethnic neighborhoods that were similar to Chinatowns, and in their own support organizations. But as hard as Japanese organizations like the Japanese-American Citizens League and the Japanese-American Organization worked to eliminate discrimination, anti-Asian sentiment grew steadily in the United States, especially (but not exclusively) on the West Coast. By 1905, San Francisco's city newspaper was running stories with such lurid headlines as "Japanese a Menace to American Women" and "The Japanese Invasion — The Problem of the Hour."

Anti-Japanese legislation halted further immigration and kept Japanese not actually born in the United States from gaining citizenship status. When white labor unions began organizing to keep Japanese workers from applying for industrial and construction jobs, Japanese-Americans turned to agriculture.

Japanese "picture brides"

The legislation passed by the U.S. government may have restricted the further immigration of Japanese males, but it did not bar entrance to the wives of men already in the United States. Most of the Japanese women who came between 1910 and 1920 arrived as "picture brides" after a marriage broker matched them with Japanese men in the United States by sending each the other's picture. The couples married — and met each other for the first time — at the piers in San Francisco and Seattle where the women disembarked from their ships. The picture brides were filled with enthusiasm, expectations, and dreams of wealth, but many met with disappointment. Men who were actually poor farm laborers sometimes borrowed an expensive suit when they had their pictures taken so their prospective brides would believe they were wealthy. Although these women had no parents nearby or anyone else they could turn to for support if their expectations fell through, most turned out to be strong and capable. If a woman's husband was a farmer, she worked the fields with him; if he owned a laundry, restaurant, or other small business, she operated it with him, seven days a week, twelve to fourteen hours a day.

But their almost immediate success as farmers created new jealousies and fears, this time among California's white farmers.

After Japan bombed Pearl Harbor in 1941 and the United States declared war on Japan, U.S. anti-Japanese paranoia reached its peak. (At the same time, however, Chinese-Americans became less detestable to white Americans, mainly because Japan and China were enemies.) On March 18, 1942, afraid that Japanese-Americans would sabotage the war effort during World War II, the U.S. government ordered that 112,000 Japanese-Americans (70,000 of whom were actually born in the United States) be removed from their homes and places of business, evacuated from the West Coast by an executive order, and placed in ten "relocation centers," where some were confined for up to four years. It was not until 1988 that the U.S. government issued a formal apology for violations of civil liberties and constitutional rights and awarded twenty thousand dollars in tax-free payments to each of the 62,500 survivors.

In 1942, afraid that Japanese-Americans would sabotage the war effort during World War II, the U.S. government ordered that 112,000 Japanese-Americans be confined for years in detention camps, like these men shown at a camp in Manzanar, California.

After World War II, overall U.S. attitudes toward Japanese-Americans changed. A major factor was how valiantly Japanese-American soldiers had fought during the war. An outstanding example is the brilliant record of the 442nd Regiment, a combat team composed almost entirely of Japanese-Americans and the most highly decorated military unit in U.S. history.

Today, Japanese-Americans are among the most assimilated of all Asian-Americans in terms of U.S. values and lifestyle. Numbering about 847,000 according to the 1990 census (600,000 on the mainland, 247,000 in Hawaii), they rank among the highest in education and income of all U.S. ethnic groups, and many among them have assumed an increasingly important role in building links between the United States and Japan.

Korean-Americans

The first Koreans to emigrate to the United States were students and political refugees fleeing their homeland in the 1880s. Large-scale immigration did not begin until 1903, when thousands of poor Korean farmers emigrated to work on Hawaiian sugar plantations. But this wave of immigrants did not last long. In 1905, when the Korean government learned of the harsh working conditions in Hawaii, it ended further emigration, so that from 1905 to 1965, only a small number of "picture brides," students, and political exiles were admitted into the United States. It was not until the U.S. quota system was abolished in 1965 that immigration from Korea again increased. By 1990, there were almost eight hundred thousand Koreans living in the United States.

While most Korean immigrants were previously engaged in professional, technical, and managerial occupations before they left Korea, many found they had to take unskilled jobs when they arrived in the United States because of language difficulties. Some started restaurants and other small businesses but found that their whole families had to work long, hard hours seven days a week, just to get by.

Filipino-Americans

In many ways, immigration from the Philippines has paralleled the Chinese and Japanese immigrations that preceded it. Early Filipino immigrants were mostly young men brought into the United States as a source of cheap labor after the Japanese were excluded in 1924. They worked mainly in seasonal agriculture in California and in salmon canneries in the Northwest and Alaska. They, too, faced racial discrimination through laws forbidding land ownership, banning of interracial marriages, and imposition of an immigration quota of only fifty per year after 1935. They were frequently refused service in restaurants and barbershops, barred from swimming pools and movies, and forced to live in slum areas.

Many Filipinos had to find work as low-paid farm laborers or as busboys, dishwashers, cooks, domestic help, and gardeners. Because of union regulations and state licensing requirements, they often found it difficult to become small businesspeople. One group that consistently found success in the United States were the *pensionados*, students on government scholarships who became professionals such as doctors or attorneys and then decided to stay in the United States rather than return to their homeland. After World War II, Filipinos found it easier to get well-paying jobs in factories, in trades, and in sales.

The number of people immigrating from the Philippines increased dramatically when quotas were lifted in 1965. Between 1960 and 1970, the Filipino-American population became the second-largest Asian-American group in the United States, following the Chinese. Many of these immigrants have been professionals and single women. In fact, by 1970, Filipino women had attained higher median levels of education that the national average for all other women.

Pacific Islander-Americans

Many Guamanians and Samoans came to the United States during the late 1930s and the 1940s by enlisting in the military services. They settled with their families mainly around U.S. military bases in the California cities of San Diego, San Francisco, and Long Beach, and in Seattle, Washington. Those who

Korean-American soldiers pause for a picture before departing on a military transport plane in 1950 for duty with General Douglas MacArthur's ground forces in South Korea. Like other Asian-Americans, Korean-Americans have fought valiantly for the United States and have a remarkable war record.

The great subcontinent

In 1947, after the end of World War II, Great Britain gave up its hold over the Indian subcontinent and the area was divided into two independent nations, India and Pakistan. In December of 1971, the eastern part of Pakistan declared itself the free and independent nation of Bangladesh. In addition to India, Pakistan, and Bangladesh, the Indian subcontinent also includes Nepal and Bhutan. (At present, the total population of the subcontinent of India is approximately 900 million people.)

have immigrated to the United States in the last few decades have been mostly younger people in search of a better life or in pursuit of higher education.

For the islanders from Hawaii, the situation was a bit different. American sugar cane planters wanted to monopolize Hawaii's immensely profitable sugar industry, and the U.S. government wanted the islands for a strategic naval base. The islands were officially annexed in 1898, and the residents of Hawaii were granted U.S. citizenship. In 1950, Hawaii become the fiftieth U.S. state.

East Indian Immigrants

The first wave of East Indian immigration, from 1901 to 1917, brought over eight thousand laborers to work in California and other Pacific Coast states. Some of these laborers worked in factories, and others entered the agricultural work force, working primarily in celery fields, citrus orchards, beet fields, and the California wine industry. Some worked on the railroads. In addition to laborers, Indian students came to attend U.S. universities. Many of these students stayed and made the United States their new home.

Most East Indian immigrants, however, did not start arriving until after Congress reformed the immigration quota system in 1965. Many of those immigrating since then have been highly educated men and women, often with special technical skills. They enter U.S. culture as professionals, especially in fields such as medicine, teaching, engineering, and science.

Very few of the first East Indians to arrive in the United States intended to remain permanently. Most saw the United States as a land of economic opportunity that would provide them with enough money to buy land (which in India means both security and status) when they returned home. Some were motivated by steamship companies and U.S. corporations that waged publicity campaigns in the East Indian lands promoting the economic opportunities the United States had to offer. Many Indians wanted to escape the poverty and terrible famines that overpopulation seemed to make worse every year. Others left for the United States to escape political discontent and increasing taxes.

Like the Chinese, East Indian workers faced almost immediate discrimination and even hostility in the United States because employers often used them as strikebreakers and because many were able to save enough to buy land and start their own businesses. This caused so much animosity among all-white, West Coast labor unions that East Indian laborers were often mobbed, stoned, and otherwise physically attacked.

Southeast Asian-Americans

Southeast Asians are the most recent immigrant group to arrive in America. The first wave consisted mainly of Cambodian, Laotian, and

In true American tradition, Laotian immigrant Duyen Baccam invites a neighboring Des Moines family to join his own in celebration of Thanksgiving. The customary roast turkey is accompanied by wonderfully spicy Laotian egg rolls and rice dishes.

Vietnamese refugees who fled from South Vietnam in 1975. These refugees settled throughout the United States, with concentrations in California, Texas, New York, and Pennsylvania, and by 1990, they numbered more than 1 million.

While many of these refugees were highly educated and had occupied important positions in government, the military, business, and industry in South Vietnam, in many cases they had to settle for low-paying, unskilled jobs. But they have shown themselves to be hard working and ambitious. Many eventually started their own businesses or studied to become professionals so that, by the early 1980s, their average household income equaled the U.S. average.

Like the Chinese and the Japanese, Southeast Asian-Americans have relied heavily on family and their own ethnic communities for support, forming organizations that offer job placement, English-language training, recreation, and other forms of mutual aid and support.

The next surge of Southeast Asian refugees started in the late 1970s. These people were mostly peasants and fishing people fleeing poverty, political prisoners finally released by the communists, or young men evading the Vietnamese draft. Escaping by sea, often aboard makeshift, overcrowded crafts, these "boat people," as they were called in the press, had to survive savage storms and lack of adequate food and water. Those who did reach Thailand or Malaysia were frequently turned away or confined to refugee camps, sometimes for years, before they received permission to emigrate to the United States.

Indian hospitality

Turn off nearly any major highway in the United States and chances are good that you will find gracious Indian hospitality. About 40 percent of all U.S. motels and smaller hotels are owned by East Indians.

Hmong immigrants

The Hmong are a small group of fiercely independent subsistence farmers who migrated in the nineteenth century into the mountains of northern Laos from China. Because they supported the United States during the Vietnam War, many Hmong families were either killed by the Vietnamese army or fled to Thailand or the United States. Many had to wait five years or more in Thai refugee camps before they were allowed to come to the United States. What has received little national attention in the United States, however, is that approximately ten thousand Hmong still remain in Thai refugee camps, waiting for permission either to emigrate to the United States or to settle in Thailand. Many Hmong-Americans are protesting the recent decision of the U.S. State Department and the Thai government to start forcing these camp refugees back to Laos, where they face persecution from the government they once fought against.

Greek immigrants settled in a variety of locales and climates when they moved to the United States in the 1800s. These men are descendants of Greek immigrants who came to Tarpon Springs, Florida, where they launched a world-famous sponge industry.

CHAPTER SEVEN

The Mediterranean and the Near and Middle East

Abraham Ahmad, a casually dressed, dark-haired businessman in his early thirties, got off the plane in London's Heathrow Airport planning to fly on to Jordon via Rome. Instead, British immigration officials seized his U.S. passport, dragged him away in handcuffs, and roughly interrogated him for the next five hours. His only crimes were his Middle Eastern appearance and the fact that his flight had arrived from Oklahoma City just hours after a massive bombing of the Oklahoma City federal building had killed more than 170 people. It was April 19, 1995.

Sadly, many Americans immediately jumped to the conclusion that Arabs must have been the perpetrators of such a terrorist act, and in their rush to bring someone to justice, they seriously violated the rights and dignity of others who are, after all, just as "American" as themselves. A former construction worker and computer technician, Ahmad was simply on a business trip — on his way to Jordon to talk to some investors about setting up a business exporting American-manufactured clothing to the Middle East.

Abraham Ahmad was not the only Arab-American whose rights were challenged; the Arab community at large became the media target of many Americans willing to stir up hatred (often to the point of inciting violence) against Americans of Middle Eastern descent. Saddened and outraged Islamic groups all over the country demanded that an apology be made to the Arab-American community, but for Ahmad and most of the others who were the direct targets of the stereotyping and rights violations, even an apology could not make up for the fear and humiliation.

Out of the Old Ottoman Empire

Like so many other Arab-Americans, Jordanian-born Abraham Ahmad came to the United States to study when he was nineteen and eventually graduated in Oklahoma with a degree in computer science. He married, applied for U.S.

As part of their annual ceremony celebrating the Feast of the Epiphany, male members of the St. Nicholas Hellenic Greek Orthodox Church dive into the icy waters off New York City's Battery Park in January 1943 to recover a gold cross thrown into the water by their archbishop.

citizenship, and settled down to raise a family in a quiet, working-class suburb of Oklahoma City. In this way, Ahmad's immigrant experience mirrored that of others whose roots reach back to the second great wave of immigrants who started arriving around 1880.

Until their defeat in World War I, the Ottoman Turks controlled an empire that stretched halfway around the Mediterranean from Greece to Turkey and Greater Syria to Northern Africa, an empire the Turks ruled with a harsh hand. During that time, the bloody struggles for independence, expanding populations, worsening economic conditions, and increasing religious and political persecution that Muslims and Christians alike had to endure at the hands of the Turks caused many residents of the Turkish empire to flee to other parts of the world. Many migrated to the United States.

Although immigrants fleeing from various parts of the Turkish empire had a lot in common when it came to their reasons for leaving, they were also from extremely diverse cultures that often harbored hatred and resentment for each other. There were deep divisions, for example, between Greeks and Albanians, Turks and Armenians, and Muslims and Christians.

Greek-Americans

Most Greeks were Christians (of the Greek Orthodox sect) and were persecuted relentlessly in the eighteenth century by their Turkish rulers — so relentlessly that a large number fled from Greece to other Mediterranean countries. Greeks did not start migrating to the United States in large numbers until the 1870s, when worsening economic conditions in their country began to reach crisis proportions. More than 80 percent of the Greek population at that time consisted of rural peasants who could barely raise enough to feed themselves on their country's stony farm fields. War with Turkey in 1897 made economic conditions even more burdensome with the sharp rise in taxes needed to pay for the war effort. The flow of Greek emigrants to the United States really started to pick up in 1890, when German and English steamship companies opened direct routes from Greece to the United States.

Like the Italians, most of the first Greek immigrants were men who wanted to make a lot of money quickly and then return home to their families. These peasants were recruited by unscrupulous Greek labor agents who promised payment for passage and used gold-in-the-streets stories to lure peasants from their homes. It was only when they found themselves in the United States on railroad construction crews, working long, backbreaking hours for almost no wages, that they realized the truth.

Most Greek immigrants moved to New England factory towns to work in textile mills and shoe factories or to other large northern cities (especially New York and Chicago), where they worked in steel mills and meat-packing plants. Many others entered service occupations or became restaurant workers. Many realized they could have an easier time making their way in the United States if they became their own bosses, so they sent for their families, worked hard, and saved enough to open shops and restaurants of their own. Some went on to become extremely successful business owners and entrepreneurs.

Greek immigrants also faced prejudice and discrimination, especially in the early years of the twentieth century, and were the targets of frequent and often bloody riots all over the United States, from Virginia to as far west as Idaho. In 1909, the Greek community of Omaha, Nebraska — about twelve hundred men, women, and children — were driven out of town and all their possessions destroyed. This anti-Greek sentiment led to the formation of organizations such as the Greek Progressive Association that worked hard to help assimilate Greek immigrants into U.S. culture and to dispel negative Greek stereotypes.

In spite of the obstacles they faced, Greek immigrants prospered as a group and made significant contributions to U.S. culture in sports, the arts, politics, and the economy. Famous second-generation Greek-Americans include opera star Maria Callas, former Vice President Spiro Agnew, actors Telly Savalas, John Cassavetes, and Betty White, and Alex Karras, an all-American defensive tackle with the Detroit Lions who also appeared in several movies.

Like many other immigrant groups, Armenians maintained strong bonds with their homeland. These enthusiastic Chicago-area Armenians organized this 1919 drive to raise money to help persecuted people starving in Armenia.

Armenian Immigrants

So many persecuted Armenian Christians have had to flee their homeland over the centuries to other countries in Europe, Asia, and Africa that when they eventually migrated to the United States, they were not counted as Armenian immigrants but were lumped instead into immigrant groups from their adopted homelands. These lands have included Turkey, Greece, Romania, Russia, Bulgaria, and Egypt.

While most Armenians fled to the U.S. to escape political oppression and mounting atrocities at the hands of other national groups, others came to escape worsening economic conditions. By 1947, the total Armenian population in the United States was estimated to be 215,000; the numbers have more than doubled again since then. Most Armenians have settled in larger cities along the East Coast.

Armenia was once a large, sprawling nation that stretched between the Black, Caspian, and Mediterranean seas. Starting in A.D. 300, however, Armenia was conquered and ruled by Assyrians, Persians, Greeks, Arabs, Persians again, and then the Ottoman Turks. Both the Persians and the Turks (who wrested Armenia from the Persians in the early 1500s) so severely oppressed their Christian subjects that Armenians began to leave their homeland and scatter throughout Europe, Asia, and Africa. In the 1800s, Russia took over a part of Armenia that later became one of the Soviet Socialist Republics. After the Russian Revolution in 1917, about 1.5 million Armenians fled Bolshevik Russia and settled in the United States and other parts of Europe. In 1915, Turkey tried to deport its entire Armenian population of 1.75 million to Syria and Palestine and then began systematically annihilating those who remained. About two hundred thousand Armenians fled Turkey to the United States. Persecution and conflict have continued into modern times. Since 1988, violent ethnic riots and armed demonstrations have been common between Armenians and neighboring Azerbaijanis. In 1991, Armenia (now just a fraction of its original, ancient size) was able to declare its independence from the Soviet Union.

Because Armenian immigrants placed a high value on education and hard work, they rose quickly to the middle and even upper classes of U.S. society, gaining high positions in industry, education, politics, and business.

Armenian immigrants have made tremendous contributions to the cultural and economic progress of the United States. Armenian-American surgeons, for example, have made significant contributions to modern medicine (surgeons like Dr. Varazted Kazanjian, who became world-renowned for his work in the development of plastic surgery after he emigrated to the United States in 1895). Armenian immigrants worked to build the nation's railroads and helped develop the tobacco, silk, and rug industries. Their history is filled with many rags-to-riches success stories such as that of tycoon Peter Paul Halajian, who founded the Peter Paul candy company in Connecticut (makers of Peter Paul Mounds and Almond Joy candy bars).

The Arabs

The word *Arab* means "those who speak clearly" and generally refers to people who speak Arabic as their native language. The term dates back to the seventh century, when all the various tribes of peoples living on the Arabian Peninsula were united by the religion of Islam, as well as by a common language.

Today, the word *Arab* refers not only to the people of the Arabian Peninsula but also to their many descendants who now populate most of the Middle East and North Africa. Most of the world's more than 100 million Arabs live in Saudi Arabia, Jordan, Qatar, Kuwait, Oman, the United Arab Emirates, Bahrain, Yemen, Iraq, Egypt, Syria, Lebanon, Libya, Algeria, Morocco, The Sudan, Tunisia, and Palestinian territories formerly occupied by Israel. Arabs also have significant communities in Chad, Iran, Turkey, and Israel. All of these Arabs consider the Arabian Peninsula (the location of their most sacred religious shrine, at the Grand Mosque in the city of Mecca) their ancestral home.

While the majority religion throughout the Arab world is Islam, there is also a substantial number of Arab Christians. In fact, most Arabs who immigrate to the United States are Christians from Lebanon or Syria.

Although a few Arabic-speaking immigrants set foot in the United States much earlier, large groups of Arabs did not start to arrive until 1865; Arabic immigration has been fairly continuous ever since. Almost all came to escape military oppression and religious persecution or to improve their family's economic condition. Nineteenth- and early twentieth-century immigrants sailed to the United States by steamship. Later arrivals came by plane.

Most Arab immigrants, Christian and Muslim alike, were from neither the elite nor the peasant classes but were merchants and small property owners from towns and villages. Many came to the United States intending to make

Family-owned Syrian delicatessens like this small shop on New York's Washington Street are still the best places to find fresh-baked *man'oushi*, a flat Syrian pita bread seasoned with *zarter*, a savory herb blend of wild marjoram, sumac, thyme, and salt.

A cradle of culture

Middle Eastern civilization, which dates back further than 3000 B.C., made brilliant contributions to world culture with the development of several major religions, technological discoveries, and inventions that include a complex writing system, paper and ink, the first 365-day calendar, and scientific medical diagnosis, as well as fine art, music, painting, architecture, and sculpture. It was the Arabs who translated Greek and Roman books on science, history, and philosophy into Arabic, thereby preserving them through the Dark Ages until they could later be translated again into European languages by twelfth-century European scholars.

The Arabs were also famous traders, carrying spices from the East Indies, silks from China, and ivory from India. Long before Europeans explored the African continent, Arabs had colonized Ethiopia, sailed down the east coast, and traded in the interior. Early European explorers like Vasco da Gama relied on the experience and advanced navigational instruments of their Arab pilots.

The beautiful architecture of Islamic mosques, like the Islamic Cultural Center of New York shown above, has enriched many U.S. cities.

a large amount of money and then return to their homelands. Other Arabs, especially Christians, fled permanently to the United States to escape persecution by the Turks. All had heard fabulous stories about the wealth and opportunity awaiting them, and, like so many other immigrants, they were shocked and dismayed at the hard economic conditions they faced when they arrived. Immigration slowed down after World War I when the Turks were defeated, until another wave started in 1930. By the late 1940s, the various countries carved out of the old Ottoman Empire had gained their independence, but the Middle East continued to be in political and economic turmoil. Since then, some Arab countries have been torn by revolution and a number of Arab leaders have been assassinated. There has also been an ongoing, bitter conflict (often including acts of terrorism) between Arabs and Israelis, centering first on the carving up of territory out of which the Jewish nation of Israel was created in 1948 and later on demands for the return of Arab land occupied by Israel and the return of Palestinians who had fled the territory. As a result, since late 1967, more than fifty thousand Arabs (many of them intellectuals) have left the Middle East for the United States.

Both Christian and Muslim Arabs brought with them a culture that emphasized hard work and discipline, an ethic that helped them overcome initial hardships. They put in long, hard hours for low pay to work their way up from peddlers, storekeepers, and laborers to become merchants, white collar workers, and professionals. Many eventually opened factories, import-export businesses, travel bureaus, steamship companies, real estate brokerages, restaurants, and bars. Two of the best known names in men's slacks — Farah and Haggar — are of Lebanese origin.

But some Americans resented the strong work ethic of Arab-Americans. Small-business owners were wary about hiring Middle Eastern employees because they were afraid the Arabs would use their employment to learn the business and then set up their own business in competition. Women were often employed in family-owned Arab businesses, a practice that was frowned upon for a long time for other American women. In many central-city neighborhoods, Arabs — especially Palestinians — have become owners of small grocery or convenience stores. Like many Korean- and East Indian-American store owners, they have often found themselves at odds with people who have lived in these central-city neighborhoods all of their lives and resent "outsiders" who come into the area to make a living and then leave for their homes elsewhere.

Religion has been another source of conflict. Some Americans were uneasy about the large number of mosques and Islamic centers that Arab-American Muslims erected in cities throughout the United States. It is not just Arab Muslims who have faced religious prejudice in the United States, however. Arab Christians have faced it, too. They brought with them the Eastern Orthodox faith, whose interpretation of Christian religion and philosophy is more oriented toward the mystical and spiritual than is Western Christianity. Because of these differences, some other Christian Americans have accused followers of the Greek Orthodox Church (as well as Roman Catholic sects such as the Melkites and Maronites) of not being true Christians.

Another stubborn source of conflict between Arab-Americans and other Americans has arisen out of the feelings of nationalism Arab immigrants continued to harbor for their homelands, especially after the creation of Israel in 1948. Organizations such as the American Arab Society, International Arab Federation, and Holy Land Fund work to keep Arab-American communities informed of liberation efforts in Arab countries, to collect funds to support those efforts, and to keep Arabic language and tradition active through newspapers and social clubs. Strong feelings of Arab nationalism are often less important, however, for many third- and fourth-generation Arab-Americans.

Lebanon's Christian majority

While most Lebanese are Arabs, less than half the population of Lebanon is Muslim. Christians make up most of the rest, making Lebanon the only Arab country with a Christian majority. The Maronite Christians are the largest Christian sect in Lebanon, and other Christian groups include Greek Orthodox and Armenian Catholic. In neighboring Syria, about 90 percent of the population belongs to Muslim sects, and only the remaining 10 percent is Christian.

Epilogue: An End to Open Doors?

When Russian-Jewish immigrant Emma Lazarus wrote for the inscription on the Statue of Liberty in 1883, "Give me your tired, your poor, your huddled masses yearning to breathe free, the wretched refuse of your teeming shore," her words reflected the philosophy of a nation that was not only made up of immigrants but was morally committed to providing hope and refuge to the poor and persecuted throughout the world.

In the 1990s, some Americans are challenging that commitment. Immigration is at one of its historic highs: Counting undocumented ("illegal") immigrants, well over 2 million people a year come to the United States, and, compared with past immigrants, far fewer of them ever leave. In fact, immigration now accounts for 37 percent of the country's population growth.

Some U.S. citizens believe that immigration has become a serious threat to this country and would like to see it stopped (or at least cut by two-thirds). They insist that instead of generating economic growth and tax revenues, immigrants are a drain on the economy because they crowd public schools, welfare rolls, hospitals, and jails. They point out that the United States is a radically different country than it was in Emma's time, that it is no longer a nation with a wide-open western frontier and a wide-open need for immigrant labor. They say the United States can no longer afford to remain a beacon of hope for the world's oppressed.

The language may be new to him, but what Russian-Jewish immigrant Thaddea Schenevitz lacks in pronunciation he more than makes up for in reverence and enthusiasm as he pledges allegiance to the U.S. flag after receiving his citizenship.

Critics of U.S. immigration policy suggest that the 1965 immigration law, which was designed to correct the injustices of previous laws, went too far the other way. By allowing large numbers of people to immigrate because they already had family members in the United States, much higher numbers of people (especially Latino people) have entered the country than were anticipated. And by also giving preference to immigrants with higher skills, they claim, the 1965 law helps take jobs away from established Americans in an already tight job market.

Immigration critics refuse to fund bilingual education, even though its purpose is to help children whose first language is not English stay in school until they know enough English to participate in a regular classroom. Yet most people would agree that without education, immigrant children have little chance of becoming successful in today's society.

Some critics of immigration also claim that the influx of cultural influences from India, the Middle East, Latin America, and Asia are "diluting" existing U.S. culture and that the United States can no longer afford to be the refuge of the world's "boat people" or political refugees from war-torn countries such as Rwanda.

At the other end of the immigration debate are those who point out that immigration has always stimulated the economy and generated a tremendous amount of tax dollars. In fact, the annual taxes paid by immigrants to all levels of government in the United States more than offset the cost of any government services they receive, generating a net surplus of $25 billion to $30 billion. Except for refugees, many say, immigrants who arrived in the past decade actually receive public assistance at significantly lower rates than U.S.-born Americans.

Americans who are pro-immigration also point out that we need immigrants because diversity is exactly what has made this nation as strong and vital as it is today. They believe the United States has a moral obligation to provide refuge for as many of the world's oppressed who choose to come here. The United States, they feel, also has a moral obligation to educate and care for innocent children, whether their parents are legal or illegal aliens, and that all children deserve an equal chance in the classroom and are therefore entitled to bilingual language assistance in public schools. They also believe that all pregnant women, whether or not they are illegal aliens, need and deserve the best prenatal care available.

Despite their strong beliefs, many people who are pro-immigration admit there are problems with the current system. Illegal immigration is the most obvious problem. One solution could be strengthening border patrols along the U.S.-Mexican border and making greater efforts to punish employers who knowingly hire illegal aliens. But a more effective solution might be to allocate federal funds to help out immigrant-swamped states like California and New York that are most heavily hit by the health, welfare, and education costs generated by both legal and illegal aliens. The way the system is set up right now, most of the economic benefits immigrants generate in a local community go to the federal government in the form of taxes, while the costs of building bigger schools and expanding health programs fall on local and state governments.

Political refugees are another important issue with no clear-cut or obvious solutions. Feeding, clothing, and sheltering large numbers of refugee families until they can find work and become self-sufficient can be extremely costly. If the United States opens its arms to all who seek refuge here, there needs to be better funded and more efficient ways of helping them assimilate, ways that do not force local communities — such as Miami in the case of its Cuban refugees — to bear the full costs.

It is interesting that critics of immigration often dredge up arguments based on all the same old prejudices and groundless stereotypes immigrants have been encountering for almost two hundred years: that immigrants are criminal, they bring diseases, they reject our culture, they refuse to learn English and assimilate, they steal our jobs, and they drain our resources. These are the same arguments used by the Know-Nothings when they violently objected to admitting the starving peasants who were fleeing Ireland's potato famine in the 1840s.

No major changes in U.S. immigration policy are likely to take place without a fuller, more informed public debate on the problem. Meanwhile, the immigration itself and all the political turmoil it creates will continue. So will the tremendous enrichment of U.S. culture and the stimulation of U.S. economy that immigration brings.

Could these be your grandparents or great-grandparents? If they immigrated through Ellis Island in 1920, they just might be.

1619	Twenty African immigrants arrive in Jamestown colony as indentured servants
1661	Slavery becomes legal in Virginia
1672	King of England charters the Royal African Company to ship slaves
1750	Slavery is now legal in all English colonies
1776	The Declaration of Independence is signed, proclaiming the birth of the United States
1808	The U.S. Constitution ends the slave trade (but not slavery)
1820	An official count of immigration begins
1830-40	The first great wave of immigration is in full swing: Northern and Western Europeans
1841-50	Thousands of Irish begin arriving in the United States, fleeing the potato famine in Ireland; the collapse of the revolutionary movement in Germany brings more immigrants; the 1948 California Gold Rush brings thousands of Chinese immigrants
1848	Treaty of Hildalgo ends the Mexican-American War, giving the U.S. most of northwestern Mexico
1851-60	Immigrants are now arriving in the United States at the rate of over 260,000 per year; Norwegian, Danish, and Swedish farmers settle in the upper Midwest
1861-65	The immigration flow decreases during the American Civil War; slavery ends
1868-78	Cuban separatists persecuted in Cuba's Ten Years War flee to the United States
1871-80	Western railroads offer reduced fares and cheap land to recruit settlers; farmers from northwestern Europe pour into the Mississippi Valley and westward; immigrant laborers dig canals, build railroads, mine minerals, cut forests, and staff industrial plants
1880	The Chinese Exclusion Act is passed, severely limiting Asian immigration for decades
1881-90	The second great wave of immigration begins: Southern and Eastern Europeans
1890-1910	The immigration of Mexicans to the United States for economic and political reasons begins; most find work in the railroad, mining, and agricultural industries
1910-20	The Mexican Revolution forces more Mexicans to migrate to the United States
1917	The end of World War I brings immigrants from war-stricken European countries
1921	Quota law passes to limit the number of European and Asian immigrants
1924	To discourage Japanese immigration, Congress bars immigration of aliens not eligible for citizenship
1941-45	The U.S. government confines Japanese-Americans to internment camps during World War II
1943	The Chinese Exclusion Act is repealed
1942-64	The Bracero program, which brings Mexican workers into the United States on temporary labor contracts, is in effect
1948	The Displaced Persons Act admits four hundred thousand European war refugees

1950-60	The first large air migration of Puerto Ricans to the mainland takes place
1950-53	The Korean War and its aftermath bring an influx of Korean refugees
1952	The Immigration and Nationality Act of 1952 (McCarran-Walter Act) reorganizes previous quota laws into one comprehensive act; in 1965, amendments to the act set up quotas by hemisphere
1965-73	African "brain drain" begins as well-educated Africans leave for the United States; Freedom Flights air lift Cuban refugees to the United States
1965-75	Immigrants from Mexico, the Philippines, Italy, and Taiwan arrive in large numbers
1978	Indochinese refugees start arriving in large numbers
1980	125,000 Cubans seek political asylum (many are "boat people")
1981-89	Almost 2.5 million people emigrate to the United States from Asia; illegal immigration becomes a growing concern in the United States
1986	The Immigration Reform and Control Act gives amnesty to illegal aliens living in the United States since 1982, creates temporary resident status for agricultural workers, and makes it illegal for employers to hire illegal aliens
1990	Reversing a trend of increasing migration to the United States by Soviet Jews, Jews from the former Soviet Union who have no relatives in the United States migrate to Israel
1991	Thousands of Haitian "boat people" seek asylum in the United States; many are denied

GLOSSARY

alien	a foreign-born resident who has not become a naturalized citizen
amnesty	government pardon for an illegal act
bracero	"day laborer"; a Mexican working in the U.S. under the Mexican Farm Labor Supply Program, a temporary agreement with Mexico (unofficially the Bracero Program), from 1942-64
Coolie	a derogatory term used to describe Chinese laborers engaged in heavy labor for little pay
Creole	a person of European descent born in areas of the West Indies, Central America, South America, or the U.S. Gulf States whose culture and dialect combine French, Spanish, Portuguese, or English; when spelled with a lowercase "c," *creole* may refer to a person whose ancestry contains a mixture of European and African influences
green card	documentation identifying foreigners with U.S. government permission to work temporarily in the United States
Hispanic	people of various ethnic backgrounds who speak a dialect of Spanish and have strong Spanish cultural influences; not a racial category but a cultural description
illegal alien	a foreign-born resident who has entered the United States without permission and is therefore subject to deportation; an undocumented worker without the green card necessary to find legal employment in the United States
indentured	bound by contract to work for a specified length of time (usually four to seven years)

internment	enforced confinement within a specific area — usually, as in the case of Japanese immigrants and Japanese-Americans interned in camps during World War II, of a group of people considered a threat to U.S. security
Middle Passage	the sea route slave ships followed across the Atlantic from Africa's Gulf of Guinea to ports in New England, the plantation South, or the West Indies
naturalization	the process of becoming a citizen of the United States
Nuyoricans	a name Puerto Ricans living in the New York City area have for themselves
quota	a set number or percentage of people of a foreign nationality allowed to immigrate into the United States in a given year
refugee	a person who flees from his or her native country to seek asylum in another country, usually to escape war or religious or political persecution
Slave Coast	a coastal area in West Africa stretching from present-day Senegal to Gambia, the Gold Coast, Guinea, and Angola from which the majority of slaves were taken for importation to North America
undocumented worker	a foreign-born resident who has entered the United States without permission and is therefore subject to deportation; a foreign worker without the green card necessary to find legal employment in the United States
"Yellow Peril"	the supposed threat to white supremacy by nineteenth- and twentieth-century Asian immigrants, especially those from Japan and China

FURTHER READING

Ashabranner, Brent K. *An Ancient Heritage: The Arab-American Minority*. New York: HarperCollins, 1991.

Cultures of America (multivolume series on U.S. ethnic groups). New York: Marshall Cavendish, 1995-1996.

Daniels, Roger. *Coming to American: A History of Immigration and Ethnicity in American Life*. New York: HarperCollins, 1990.

Hamanaka, Sheila. *The Journey: Japanese Americans, Racism and Renewal*. New York: Orchard Books, 1990.

Hoflund, Charles J. *Getting Ahead: A Swedish Immigrant's Reminiscences, 1834-1887*. Carbondale: Southern Illinois University Press, 1989.

Holland, F. Ross. *Idealists, Scoundrels, and the Lady: An Insider's View of the Statue of Liberty-Ellis Island Project*. Urbana: University of Illinois Press, 1993.

Klevan, Miriam. *The West Indian Americans*. New York: Chelsea House, 1990.

Mesa-Lago, Carmelo. *Cuba's Raft Exodus of 1994: Causes, Settlement, Effects, and Future*. Coral Gables: North-South Center, University of Miami, 1995.

Muller, Thomas. *Immigrants and the American City*. New York: New York University Press, 1993.

Nolan, Janet. *Ourselves Alone: Women's Emigration from Ireland, 1885-1920*. Lexington: University Press of Kentucky, 1989.

Nraunstein, Susan L., ed. *Getting Comfortable in New York: The American Jewish Home, 1880-1950*. New York: The Jewish Museum, 1990.

Portes, Alejandro. *Immigrant America: A Portrait*. Berkeley: University of California Press, 1990.

Reimers, David M. *Still the Golden Door: The Third World Comes to America*. New York: Columbia University Press, 1992.